FRIENDS
OF ACPL

3/10

Paper Plate
Christian Crafts

PARENT-TEACHER COLLECTION

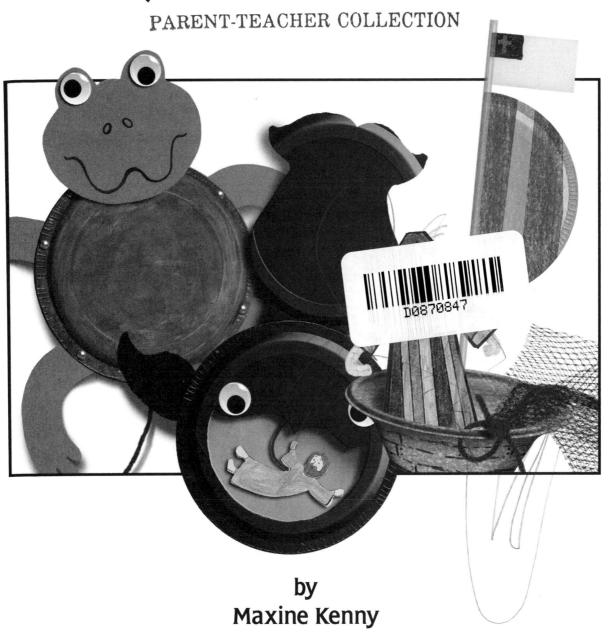

by
Maxine Kenny

Carson-Dellosa Publishing Company, Inc.
Greensboro, North Carolina

It is the mission of Carson-Dellosa to create the highest-quality
Scripture-based children's products that teach the Word of God,
share His love and goodness, assist in faith development,
and glorify His Son, Jesus Christ.

"Teach me your ways so I may know you."
Exodus 33:13

Credits

Editor: Carol Layton
Layout Design: Nick Greenwood
Inside Illustrations: Maxine Kenny
Cover Design: Nick Greenwood
Cover Photography: © Shutterstock.com

Unless otherwise noted, all Scripture is taken from the HOLY BIBLE, NEW INTERNATIONAL VERSION. Copyright © 1973, 1978, 1984 by International Bible Society. Used by permission of Zondervan Bible Publishers.

Scripture marked NLT is taken from the Holy Bible, New Living Translation, copyright 1996. Used by permission of Tyndale House Publishers, Inc., Wheaton, Illinois 60189. All rights reserved.

© 2008, Carson-Dellosa Publishing Company, Inc., Greensboro, North Carolina 27425. The purchase of this material entitles the buyer to reproduce worksheets and activities for classroom use only—not for commercial resale. Reproduction of these materials for an entire school or district is prohibited. No part of this book may be reproduced (except as noted above), stored in a retrieval system, or transmitted in any form or by any means (mechanically, electronically, recording, etc.) without the prior written consent of Carson-Dellosa Publishing Co., Inc.

Printed in the USA • All rights reserved.

ISBN 978-1-60022-521-5

Table of Contents

Teaching (and having fun!) with Paper Plates 5

Helpful Information 6

Old Testament

God's Lights in the Sky: *Spinner Toy* 7

God's Little Creatures: *Animal Toys* 9

God Made You Special: *Hand Mirror* 11

The Cunning Snake in the Garden of Eden: *Spiral Spinner* 12

Garden of Eden: *Dry Dish Garden* 13

Noah's Ark: *Rocking Ark* 16

Abram Counts the Stars: *Mobile* 18

Joseph's Robe of Many Colors: *Stringed Puppet* 21

Baby Moses: *Jointed Doll* 24

Plague of Frogs: *Leaping Frog* 27

God Saves the Israelites: *Parting Sea Plate* 30

Moses and the Ten Commandments: *Talking Puppet* 33

Samson the Strong Man: *Double Masks* 35

David's Fight with Goliath: *Action Toy* 37

Elijah Fed by Ravens: *Toss and Catch Game* 40

God Cares for You: *Wheel of Faces* 42

Guardian Angel: *Doorknob Hanger* 44

God Cares for His Animals: *Wall Pockets* 45

Praise God: *Tambourine* 47

Peacemakers: *Lion and Lamb Caddies* 48

Three Men in a Fiery Furnace: *Pull-Tab Toy* 51

Daniel in the Lions' Den: *Jigsaw Puzzle* 54

Jonah in the Big Fish: *Mobile* 56

New Testament

Jesus' Birth through Choosing the Disciples

Jesus Is Born: *Stand-Up Nativity Figures* 59

Happy Birthday, Jesus: *Pretend Cake* 62

Magi Follow the Star: *Story Wheel* 64

Gifts of the Magi: *Potpourri Container* 67

Jesus' Baptism: *Flying Dove* 68

Table of Contents

The First Disciples: *Fishing Boat* 71

Fishers of Men: *Magnetic Fishing Game* 73

Teachings of Jesus

God Loves the World: *Medallion* 75

Shine for Jesus: *Wall Plaque* 76

God Cares for You: *Flowered Hat* 78

Christian Symbols: *Sun Catcher* 80

The Good Shepherd: *Game Board* 83

Prodigal's Pig: *Piggy Bank* 85

Jesus Loves You This Much!: *Greeting Card* 88

Smile, Jesus Loves You!: *Paddle Ball Game* 91

Love Your Neighbor: *Friend Fan* 93

Miracles of Jesus

A Net Full of Fish: *Wall Plaque* 95

Jesus Heals a Paralyzed Man: *Walking Figure* 97

Jesus Calms the Winds: *Wind Sock* 99

Jairus's Daughter: *Stick Puppet* 100

Jesus Feeds the Hungry People: *Pop-Up Toy* 102

Jesus Walks on Water: *Magnet Walk Toy* 105

In the Garden and the Risen Jesus

Garden of Gethsemane: *Dry Dish Garden* 108

Jesus Arose: *Dry Dish Garden* 111

Soar with Jesus: *Discus* 114

Paul's Teachings

I Am a New Creation!: *Butterfly Wand* 116

Jesus Loves a Cheerful Giver: *Gift Box* 119

Open Your Heart to Jesus: *Greeting Card* 121

Multi-Use Projects

Bible Story Theater and Puppets 124

Angel Messenger: *Hand Puppet* 126

Teaching (and having fun!) with Paper Plates

These imaginative toys, games, and crafts will delight children with their movement and interaction. You'll be delighted too with how easy and inexpensive they are to make! What could be better than that? Lots! While playing with each project and using the provided teaching during the construction, children will grow in God's love and gain a better understanding of the Bible!

Each project includes:

- **Mini-lesson**
  Use these discussion starters while children work on their projects. Engage children with questions about each Bible story and what it means to them.

- **Suggested uses**
  These offer extra ideas for using each project or ways to increase its ministry value.

- **Scripture reference**
  Each project is based on a specific Bible story, Scripture, or theme. Enhance each project by reading and discussing these passages before children begin their projects.

- **Memory verse**
  Each project also includes a child-friendly memory verse that can be incorporated into the making or use of the project.

- **Instructions**
  Step-by-step instructions, illustrations, complete materials lists, and reproducible patterns are provided for the projects. Paper plates and bowls are the main materials needed, but additional craft supplies are inexpensive and easy to obtain. Preview each craft to see if certain steps should be completed prior to class time. This may benefit younger children.

Let the fun and learning begin!

Helpful Information

Paper plates and bowls come in various sizes, materials, and strengths. Unless otherwise specified, use uncoated paper plates and bowls since crayons, markers, and paints do not adhere to foam, waxed, or plastic-coated products. Uncoated paper plates and bowls are less expensive, are easy to cut, and provide a white surface on which to color.

Plates

The following types of plates are used:

Flexible plates:	Use uncoated regular paper plates.
Sturdy plates:	Use uncoated, two-ply paper plates or glue two flexible plates together.
Dinner plates:	9" or 10" (23 or 25 cm)
Dessert plates:	7" (18 cm)
Oval platters:	9.5" x 12" (24 x 30 cm)
Paper bowls:	12 oz. (340 g)
Plastic bowls:	12 oz. (340 g)

To Find the Center of Plates

An easy way to find the center of a plate is to fold a flexible plate in half, crease it, then unfold and fold in half again from the opposite direction. With a pencil, mark where the two creases intersect. To find the center of a plate without folding it, place a plate with a hole punched in the center on top of the plate. Mark the center with a pencil.

Reproducing the Patterns

The full-size patterns in this book may be reproduced on a photocopier for classroom use.

Express Yourself!

With the basic patterns given, children can still express their creativity by using different colors and designs. Encourage children to use their own ideas and imaginations while creating the projects.

God's Lights in the Sky

Genesis 1:14-19

God made two great lights, the greater light the sun for the day, and the lesser light the moon for the night. He also made the stars. Remind children to always let their light shine for God. Discuss the special gift that each child has for expressing God's light and love to the world.

Memory Verse

And God said, "Let there be lights in the expanse of the sky to separate the day from the night."
Genesis 1:14

Materials

- One sturdy dinner-size paper plate
- Scissors
- Paper hole punch
- Poster board (white)
- Crayons, markers, or paints
- Four 12" (30 cm) pieces of string
- One unsharpened pencil
- One thumbtack or pushpin
- Glue

Roll the pencil between your hands to remember God's beautiful lights in motion.

Suggested Uses

1. Alternatively, simply suspend the cutouts from a paper plate to make a mobile.
2. Have children say the memory verse as they spin the toy.

Directions

1. Cut away the rim of a sturdy dinner-size paper plate to make a paper circle.
2. Use a paper hole punch to make four equally spaced holes around the edge of the circle. Then write "God's Lights" on the circle.
3. Copy and cut out the patterns on page 8. Glue the patterns onto poster board. Decorate the reverse side of each cutout.
4. Punch a hole at the top of each cutout.
5. Tie one end of each string to a cutout and the other end of each string to a hole in the paper circle. Cut off excess string.
6. Use a thumbtack to attach the paper circle at its center to the eraser of an unsharpened pencil. (This step should be completed by an adult or with adult supervision.)

God's Little Creatures

Genesis 1: 24-25

God loves and cares for all of His creatures. He gives them hard shells and stingers to protect themselves. He gives them foods to nourish them. Ask children to think of other ways that God cares for every living thing.

Memory Verse

God said, "Let the land produce living creatures according to their kinds."

Genesis 1:24

Materials

- One paper cereal bowl
- Ruler
- Scissors
- Two empty thread spools for rollers (optional)
- Two pipe cleaners
- Paper hole punch
- Crayons, markers, or paints
- Construction paper scraps
- Glue

These toys can move on rollers to imitate God's little creatures.

Suggested Uses

1. Have children make a bee, spider, turtle, or ladybug. Then, mark off a track on a sloping surface and allow them to race their creatures.

2. Children can give the creatures as gifts to friends.

Optional Materials

- Legs: chenille craft sticks, yarn, or felt
- Antennae: pipe cleaners
- Mouths: yarn
- Eyes: plastic wiggle eyes
- Spider hair: craft fur
- Wings: waxed paper

Directions

These directions are the same for the bee, spider, turtle, and ladybug.

1. Cut away the rim of a paper bowl for the body. Turn the bowl over and color the back of your chosen creature. Glue construction paper cutouts to the body to make a head, eyes, mouth, legs, wings, and antennae. Or, glue on some of the optional materials.

2. To allow the creatures to roll (optional), use a paper hole punch to make two holes on each side of the bowl. Holes should be about 0.25" (0.6 cm) from the rim (fig. 1).

3. To allow the creatures to roll (optional), each creature will need two thread spools. To make each roller, insert one end of a chenille craft stick into a hole in the bowl, thread into the thread spool, then push the craft stick into the hole on the opposite side of the bowl. Wrap the ends of the craft stick around themselves inside the body to secure (fig. 2).

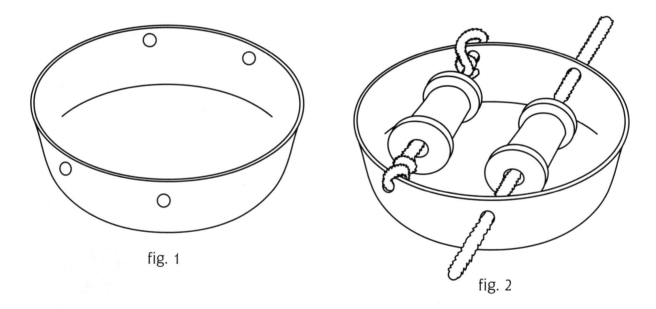

fig. 1

fig. 2

God Made You Special

Genesis 1:26-27

God created us in His very own image! And, just like snowflakes, no two of us are exactly alike! God made each of us with special gifts and abilities so that we can play unique roles in His Kingdom and be unique expressions of His love.

Memory Verse

God created people in His own image.

Genesis 1:27 NLT

Use this mirror to remind children that they were made in God's image.

Suggested Uses

1. Have children look in their mirrors as they draw pictures of themselves.

2. Have children repeat the memory verse together.

Materials

- One sturdy dessert paper plate
- Plastic mirror, 3" (8 cm) round (or foil)
- Glue
- Jumbo craft stick
- Yarn (various colors)
- Scissors
- Ribbons, hair clips, etc. (optional)

Directions

1. Glue the mirror in the center of a dessert-size plate (eating side). Allow to dry.

2. Glue a jumbo craft stick to the middle of the back of the plate to make a handle.

3. Choose yarn similar to hair color. Cut the yarn and glue pieces around the mirror and on the back of the plate to make hair. When dry, style the hair and add accessories if desired.

The Cunning Snake in the Garden of Eden

Hang the spiral snake as a reminder to obey God.

Suggested Uses

1. Have children write "Obey God" on their snakes, then wrap the snakes around their arms to share the message with others.

2. Have children use the snakes to reenact the story of Paul on the island of Malta. (Acts 28:1–6)

Satan appeared as a snake in the garden and lied to Eve. God told the snake, "You will crawl on your belly and you will eat dust all the days of your life." Satan will always lie because he is the "father of lies." Encourage children to listen to God, to trust Him only, and not to pay attention to the lies of the devil.

Memory Verse

The serpent was more crafty than any of the wild animals the Lord God had made.

Genesis 3:1

Materials

- One flexible dinner-size paper plate
- Crayons, markers, or paints
- Pencil
- Ruler
- Scissors
- Two plastic wiggle eyes (optional)
- Glue
- Paper hole punch
- Yarn

Directions

1. Decorate both sides of a flexible dinner-size plate.

2. With a pencil, draw spiral lines on the eating side of the plate (fig. 1).

3. Cut the plate into a spiral by starting at the rim and cutting around and around, following the pencil lines.

4. The center of the plate forms the head. Color dots for eyes or use plastic wiggle eyes. Cut a forked tongue from a plate scrap and glue onto the mouth.

5. With a paper hole punch, make a hole at the top of the snake's head. Tie a piece of yarn through the hole for hanging.

fig. 1

Garden of Eden

Genesis 3:1-24

Adam and Eve disobeyed God when they ate the forbidden fruit in the Garden of Eden, but God still loved them.

Memory Verse

The Lord God said, "The man has now become like one of us, knowing good and evil."

Genesis 3:22

Materials

- One sturdy dinner-size paper plate or platter
- Scissors
- Pencil
- Crayons, markers, or paints
- Poster board (white)
- Glue

This garden illustrates where man and woman began and why they had to leave the garden.

Suggested Uses

1. Children can tell others about the story they depict in their dry dish gardens.

2. Have children use the gardens for table decorations or to give as gifts.

Optional Landscape Materials

- Treetops: Glue on cotton balls for foliage. Paint the cotton balls green by rubbing them with a green marker. For a fruit tree, glue on fruits cut from construction paper.

- Boulder: pebble or painted crumpled paper

- Pond, Lake, or Stream: blue construction paper covered with clear plastic wrap, aluminum foil, or small pocket mirror

- Grass: bits of green tissue paper, crushed crepe paper, finely shredded Easter grass, bits of green construction paper, or curled paper ribbon

- Flowers: tiny plastic or silk flowers

- Butterfly: Cut a tiny butterfly from tissue paper. Glue it to a toothpick.

- Snake: Cut and glue a green construction paper head to green chenille craft stick.

- Ground Covers: sand, sieved soil, sawdust

Garden of Eden (continued)

1. Plan your garden carefully. Gather the optional landscape materials you may want to use in your garden to go along with your stand-up cutouts.

2. Copy the patterns on page 15. Cut out the patterns and glue them onto poster board.

3. Arrange the patterns and the optional landscape materials on a large dinner plate or platter in an interesting arrangement. When you have decided on an arrangement, fold back the tabs and glue the patterns in place (fig. 1). Glue the other materials in place.

4. Once the stand-ups and other materials are glued in place, coat the inside of the plate or platter with a generous layer of glue and sprinkle or press on some of the optional ground covers. You may prefer to paint a ground cover instead.

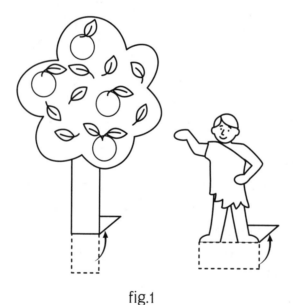

fig.1

Garden of Eden Patterns

Noah's Ark

Rocking Ark

Rock the ark while telling the story of Noah's ark and the great flood.

Suggested Uses

1. Have children tell the story of Noah in their own words as they rock the boat.

2. Have children discuss God's promise not to send another flood to destroy the earth.

God saw that everyone on the earth had become evil. He told Noah to build an ark before a great flood came to wash the world clean for a new beginning. Noah obeyed God in every detail. Encourage children to obey God like Noah did.

Memory Verse

Noah did everything just as God commanded him.

Genesis 6:22

Materials

- One flexible dinner-size paper plate
- Ruler
- Pencil
- Crayons, markers, or paints
- Glue
- Scissors
- Poster board (white)
- Tape

Directions

1. Lightly fold a flexible dinner-size plate in half and then unfold it.

2. Use a ruler to draw two straight lines about one inch from each side of the fold.

3. Fold the plate along each of the lines to make a rocker.

4. Color the rocker to look like water.

5. Copy the ark pattern on page 17. Cut out and glue the pattern onto poster board. Color the ark.

6. Cut two slits at the top-center of the rocker and insert the tabs at the bottom of the ark. Bend the ends of the tabs and tape them underneath (in opposite directions) to keep the ark upright.

Noah's Ark Pattern

Abram Counts the Stars

Mobile

This mobile is a reminder of God's promise to Abram to make his descendants as numerous as the stars.

Suggested Uses

1. Alternatively, children can cut out the figure of Abram and glue it to a dinner-size paper plate. Color Abram, the sky, and the ground. Fill the sky with star stickers and glue dry sand on the ground.

2. Have children create mobiles to depict other Bible stories.

When Abram and his wife were very old, God promised to give him more descendants than all of the stars Abram could count. Abram believed God's promise, and that made God very happy. Encourage children to always believe God's promises because He always keeps them!

Memory Verse

"Look up at the heavens and count the stars. . . . So shall your offspring be."

Genesis 15:5

Materials

- Two sturdy dinner-size plates
- Pencil
- Scissors
- Glue
- Poster board (white)
- Crayons, markers, or paints
- Glitter
- Paper hole punch
- Yarn

Directions

1. Draw a line to form a crescent-shaped moon on the eating side of a sturdy dinner-size paper plate (fig. 1). Cut out. Place the cutout moon inside a second dinner-size plate and trace around the cut edge to make another moon shape. Cut out.

2. Color both sides of the moon cutouts, then glue the two moon shapes together, rim-to-rim, with the eating sides facing inward (fig. 2).

3. Copy the patterns on page 20. Cut out and glue onto poster board.

4. Spread a layer of glue over both sides of each star and sprinkle with glitter to add sparkle.

5. Color both sides of the Abram pattern and each of the star patterns.

6. Use a paper hole punch to make one hole at the top of the moon, five holes along the inside curve of the moon, one hole from which to hang Abram, one hole at the top of each star, and one hole at the top of Abram.

7. Cut five pieces of yarn into different lengths (6–12", 15–30 cm). Use the yarn to hang the stars and Abram from the moon at different levels. Thread the yarn through the holes and knot the ends. Place spots of glue on the knots for added strength.

8. Cut a long piece of yarn and tie through the hole at the top of the moon for hanging.

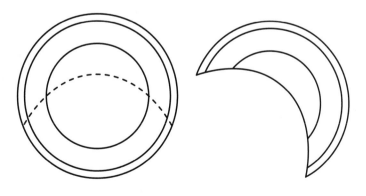

fig. 1   fig. 2

Abram Counts the Stars Patterns

Joseph's Robe of Many Colors

Genesis 37:1–11

Israel (Jacob) made his son Joseph a beautiful robe. Joseph's brothers' jealousy kept them from being blessed and caused them many years of trouble. Encourage children to be happy when they see others blessed, knowing that God will always have special blessings for them too!

Memory Verse

Israel loved Joseph . . . because he had been born to him in his old age; and he made a richly ornamented robe for him.

Genesis 37:3

Use the puppet to reenact the story of Joseph.

Suggested Uses

1. Have children tell the story of Joseph as they make the puppet jump or walk.

2. Ask children to tell about their favorite articles of clothing.

Materials

- Two sturdy dessert-size paper plates
- Two sturdy dinner-size paper plates
- Yarn
- Scissors
- Glue
- Pencil
- Poster board (white)
- Crayons, markers, or paints
- Paper hole punch
- Two plastic wiggle eyes (optional)
- Two sheets of construction paper (white)
- One 12" (30 cm) piece of elastic

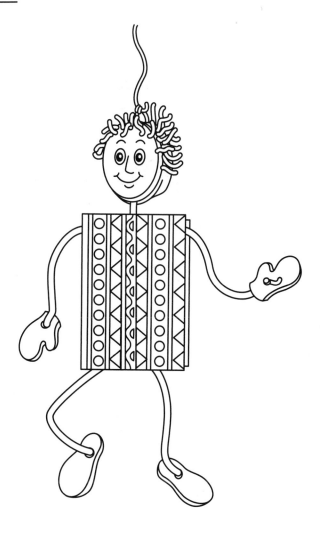

Directions

1. Glue one end of a 3" (8 cm) piece of yarn to the inside rim of a dessert-size plate for a neck. Glue pieces of yarn on the head for hair. Glue a second dessert-size plate on top, rim-to-rim (eating sides facing inward), to make a head (fig. 1).

2. Cut two 8" (20 cm) pieces of yarn for arms and two 12" (30 cm) pieces for legs.

3. Glue the other end of the neck, and the arms and legs into position on the inside rim of the eating side of a dinner-size plate. Glue another dinner-size plate on top, rim-to-rim (eating sides facing inward), to make a body (fig. 2).

4. Copy the hand and shoe patterns on page 23. Cut out the patterns and glue onto poster board to make two hands and two shoes. Color both sides of the hands and shoes.

5. Use a paper hole punch to make a hole in each hand and shoe. Then, thread the yarn arms and legs through the holes and tie. Put a spot of glue on top of each knot for added strength.

6. Color the face. Add eyes, eyebrows, a nose, and a big smile. Color the eyes or glue on plastic wiggle eyes.

7. Decorate the white sheets of construction paper with colorful designs to make the front and back of a colorful robe.

8. Glue the robe pieces to the front and back of the body.

9. Punch a hole at the top of the head and thread the piece of elastic through the hole and tie.

10. To make the Joseph puppet jump for joy, hold the end of the elastic and bounce him up and down.

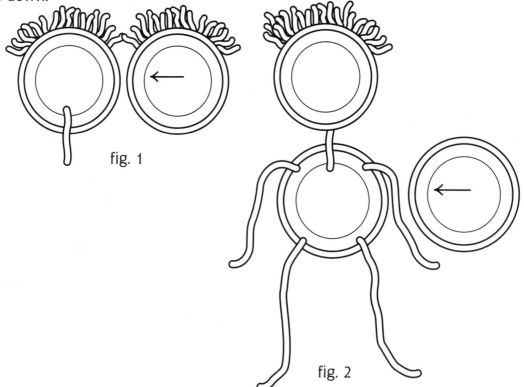

fig. 1

fig. 2

Joseph's Robe of Many Colors Patterns

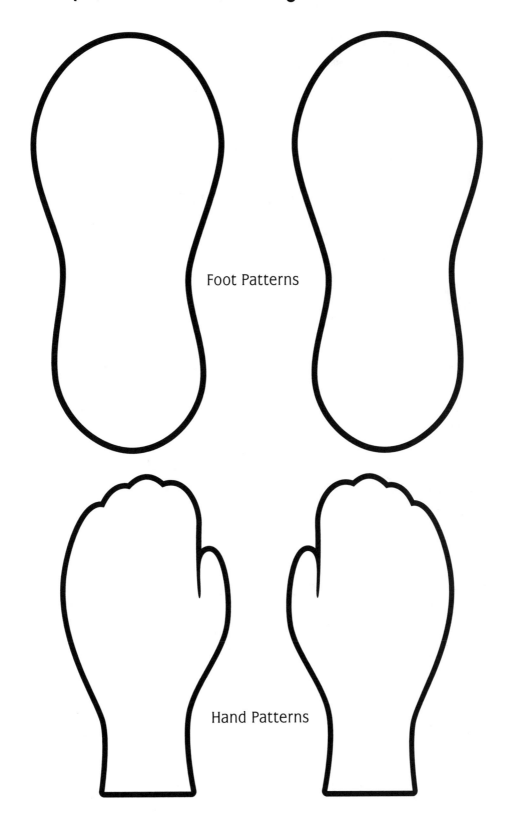

Foot Patterns

Hand Patterns

Baby Moses

Use this doll to tell the story of God taking care of baby Moses.

Suggested Uses

1. Have children place the Moses doll in a basket and tell the story of how he was found.

2. Children can use the doll to tell stories of other Bible babies:

   Isaac–Genesis 21:1–7

   Samuel–1 Samuel 1:20–28

   John the Baptist–
   Luke 1:11–14

   Jesus–Luke 2:1–7

Moses' parents weren't afraid of the Pharaoh's command. (Hebrews 11:23) They showed their faith by placing baby Moses in a basket and hiding him among the reeds along the Nile River. God honored their faith and sent a princess to rescue their baby.

Memory Verse

She named him Moses, saying, "I drew him out of the water."

Exodus 2:10

Materials

- Four sturdy dessert-size paper plates
- Ruler
- Pencil
- Scissors
- Poster board (white)
- Paper hole punch
- Glue
- Paper clips
- Five brass paper fasteners
- Crayons, markers, or paints
- Yarn

Directions

1. Cut off about 0.25" (1 cm) from around the rims of two sturdy dessert-size plates to make a front and back for the baby's head. Do not glue together.

2. Trace the neck pattern on page 26 onto poster board. Cut out. Use a paper hole punch to make a hole where the pattern indicates.

3. Glue the neck to the rim (eating side) of one of the plates used to make the head (fig. 1).

4. Put glue around the edge of the other plate and place it, rim-to-rim, (with the eating sides facing inward) onto the plate with the neck (fig. 2). Hold it in place with paper clips until dry.

5. Trace the arm and leg patterns onto poster board. Cut out and punch holes where the patterns indicate.

6. Punch three holes in a third dessert-size plate (fig. 3). Attach the neck and the legs to the plate with brass paper fasteners so that the shanks of the fasteners are opened on the eating side of the plate (fig. 4).

7. Punch two holes in a fourth dessert-size plate (fig. 5). Attach the arms to the plate with brass paper fasteners so that the shanks are opened on the eating side of the plate (fig. 6).

8. Glue the plate with the arms onto the plate with the legs, rim-to-rim, eating sides facing. (Be careful not to glue the areas around each fastener so that the head, arms, and legs can move freely.) Hold in place with paper clips until dry.

9. The front of the baby is the side where only two fasteners are visible on the arms. Color both sides of the baby and add facial features. Glue on yarn for hair.

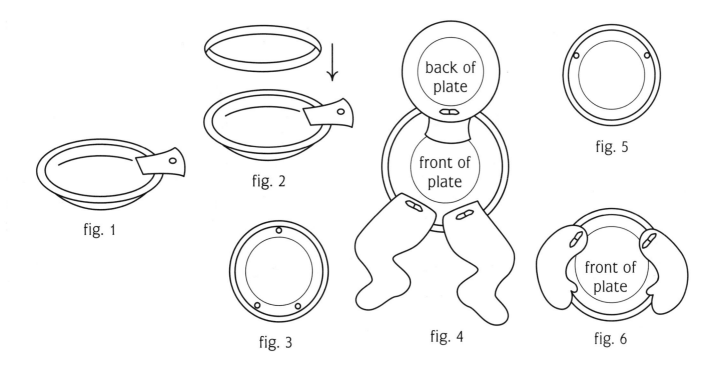

fig. 1

fig. 2

fig. 3

fig. 4

fig. 5

fig. 6

Baby Moses Patterns

Leg Patterns

Neck Pattern

Arm Patterns

Plague of Frogs

Exodus 8:1-14

The Pharaoh was hard-hearted because he continually disobeyed God. Many plagues came upon the people of Egypt until the Pharaoh finally agreed to let the Israelites go. Encourage children to always obey God and their parents. Obedience will keep their hearts nice and soft!

Memory Verse

"Let my people go, so that they may worship me."

Exodus 8:1

Materials

- One sturdy dinner-size plate
- Construction paper (green)
- Pencil
- Scissors
- Crayons, markers, or paints
- Glue
- Two plastic wiggle eyes (optional)
- Paper hole punch
- Four brass paper fasteners
- Yarn
- Bead (optional)

Leaping Frog

Use the frog to tell the story of God sending a plague of frogs over the land of Egypt to free the Israelites.

Suggested Uses

1. Teach children an acronym for FROG: Fully Rely on God. How did Moses fully rely on God? On whom did the Pharaoh rely?

2. Have children repeat the words, "Leap for the Lord!" as they make the frog jump.

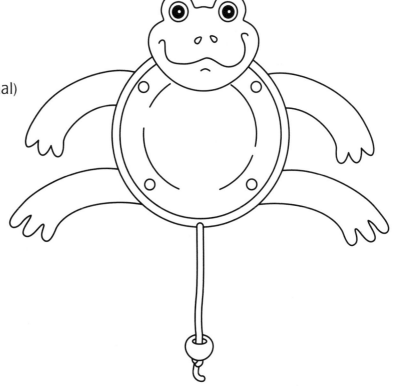

Directions

1. Trace the frog patterns on page 29 onto green construction paper. Make two arms and two legs.

2. Decorate the face by adding a mouth, nostrils, and eyes. Or, glue on plastic wiggle eyes.

3. Color the non-eating side of a dinner-size plate for the body.

4. Use a paper hole punch to make four holes in the body (fig. 1) and one hole at the top corner and one hole at the top center of each arm and leg (fig. 2).

5. Glue the head to the decorated side of the body.

6. Attach the arms and legs to the body by inserting a brass paper fastener through the hole in the center of each arm and leg. (Keep the fasteners loose enough so that the arms and legs can move up and down easily.)

7. Cut three 12" (30 cm) pieces of yarn. Thread one piece of yarn through the holes in the top corners of the arms at the top of the frog and tie the ends together. Do the same with the legs at the bottom of the frog (fig. 3).

8. Tie the third piece of yarn to the pieces of yarn between each set of legs (fig. 4). Pull the third piece of yarn to make the frog leap. To make it easier to pull, thread a bead onto the end of the yarn and secure it with a knot.

9. Hold the frog in one hand and with the other hand pull gently on the yarn to make the frog leap.

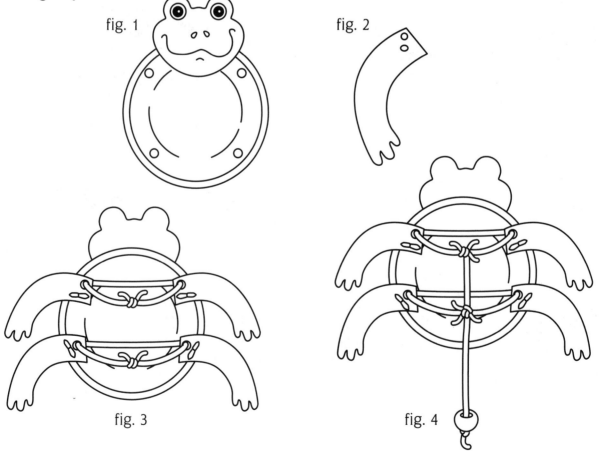

fig. 1

fig. 2

fig. 3

fig. 4

Plague of Frogs Patterns

Frog Head Pattern

Arms and Legs Pattern

God Saves the Israelites

Part the Red Sea to reveal God's people walking on dry ground!

Suggested Uses

1. Have children write skits about what the characters say as they walk through the dry seabed.

2. Have children say the memory verse each time they "part the waters."

When the Red Sea parted, it was a mighty miracle, but Moses had a part to play in it. Before the miracle happened, Moses had to stretch out his hand as God commanded. Encourage each child to be ready to do his part as he trusts God for miracles.

Memory Verse

The Israelites went through the sea on dry ground, with a wall of water on their right and on their left.

Exodus 14:22

Materials

- Two dinner-size plates (flexible or sturdy)
- Ruler
- Pencil
- Fine-line markers (variety of colors)
- Paper hole punch
- Glue
- Scissors
- Two brass paper fasteners

Directions

1. Decorate a dinner-size plate to resemble water. Use a pencil and ruler to draw a straight line down the center of the non-eating side of the plate.

2. Copy the patterns on page 32. Cut out the patterns and color them.

3. Glue the fish onto both sides of the line, but not touching the line (fig. 1). Cut the plate in half using the marked pencil line as a guide.

4. Decorate the eating side of the second plate to resemble sand. Glue the people onto the sand.

5. Put the halves with the fish on top of the plate with the people, rim-to-rim (with the eating sides facing inward). Hold the plates together and use a paper hole punch to make holes through the bottoms of both plates. Put brass paper fasteners through the holes to hold the plates together.

6. Open and close the plate halves to show the parting of the Red Sea (fig. 2).

fig. 1

fig. 2

God Saves the Israelites Patterns

Moses and the Ten Commandments

Exodus 20:3–17

Moses went up the mountain and talked with God. When he came down the mountain, he carried two stone tablets upon which God had written 10 good rules for us to live by—the Ten Commandments.

Memory Verse

The LORD said. . . . "Obey what I command you today."

Exodus 34:10–11

Materials

- One sturdy dinner-size paper plate
- One cardboard paper towel tube
- Crayons, markers, or paints
- Two large plastic wiggle eyes (optional)
- Two brass paper fasteners
- One large rubber band
- String, 20" (50 cm)
- Scissors
- Glue
- Cotton balls

Talking Puppet

Pull a string to let the Moses puppet talk about the Ten Commandments.

Suggested Uses

1. Have children use the puppet to put on a show reciting the Ten Commandments. (See Exodus 20:1–17.)

2. Children can use the puppet to have Moses tell the story of how his mother hid him in a basket. (See Exodus 2:1–10.)

Directions

1. Decorate the non-eating side of a sturdy dinner-size plate and a cardboard paper towel tube to make a head and neck for the puppet.

2. Color a nose and eyes on the paper plate. Plastic wiggle eyes can be glued to the head instead of drawn eyes. (Do not make a mouth.)

3. To form a mouth, insert two brass paper fasteners near the bottom of the plate where the corners of the mouth will be. Hook a rubber band over the two fasteners. Tie one end of a 20" (51 cm) piece of yarn to the lower half of the rubber band (fig. 1).

4. Cut a vertical 1" (2.5 cm) slits on each side of the top of the cardboard tube. Drop the other end of the string into the tube so that it falls through the bottom. Then, slide the head into the slits (fig. 2).

5. Glue cotton balls to the face for eyebrows, hair, and a beard (fig. 3).

6. To make the Moses puppet "talk," pull gently on the end of the yarn to move his mouth.

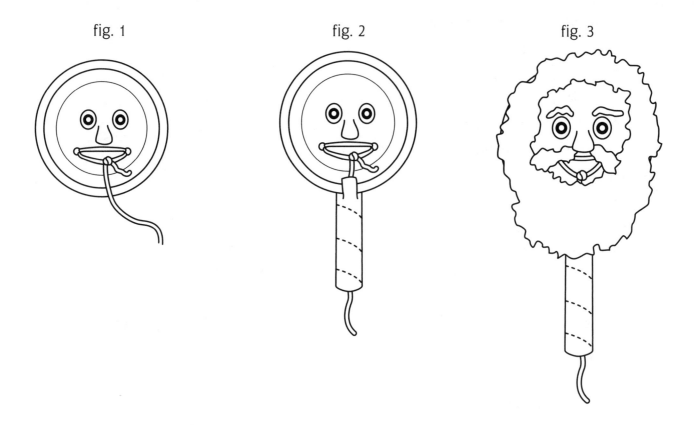

fig. 1   fig. 2   fig. 3

Samson the Strong Man

Judges 16:17-30

When Samson prayed to God, his great strength returned and he was able to help God save the Israelites from their enemies. Remind children that God is always ready to renew us and cleanse us when we repent of our sins.

Memory Verse

Then Samson prayed to the Lord . . . "Please strengthen me just once more."

Judges 16:28

Materials

- Two flexible dinner-size paper plates
- Pencil
- Ruler
- Scissors
- Stapler
- Glue
- Crayons, markers, or paints
- Yarn
- Thin elastic
- Tape

Wear the masks to illustrate what happened to the mighty Samson when he disobeyed God.

Suggested Uses

1. Have children wear the masks and turn their bodies from front to back while pretending to be Samson and telling Samson's story.

2. Have children make masks of other Bible characters to act out other Bible stories.

Directions

Two plates are needed to make two masks. The front part of the mask shows Samson strong and happy with hair. The back part of the mask shows Samson weak and sad with his head shaven.

1. On each plate, cut two diagonal slits along the rim about 1" (2.5 cm) deep and about 3" (8 cm) apart to make the masks three-dimensional and to fit the face (fig. 1). Overlap the slits and staple closed to form a chin (fig. 2).

2. Hold each of the two masks against a child's face and use a crayon to lightly mark the position of eyes and nose. Remove the plates and draw circles for eyes on one of the masks large enough for full vision. Cut out the circles. On the other mask (which will go at the back of the head) draw eyes but do not cut them out (fig. 3).

3. Cut a small slit at the nostril line for the nose. This will allow the plate to bend to form around nose.

4. Color the masks. On the mask with the cutout circles for eyes, draw happy features (fig. 4) and on the other mask draw sad features (fig. 5).

5. Cut long pieces of yarn for hair and glue them to the happy Samson mask. Do not glue hair on the sad Samson mask.

6. To keep the masks on the head, cut two equal pieces of thin elastic. Staple one end of a piece of elastic to the side of one mask. Staple the other end of the elastic to the side of the other mask. Do the same on the other sides of the masks with the second piece of elastic.

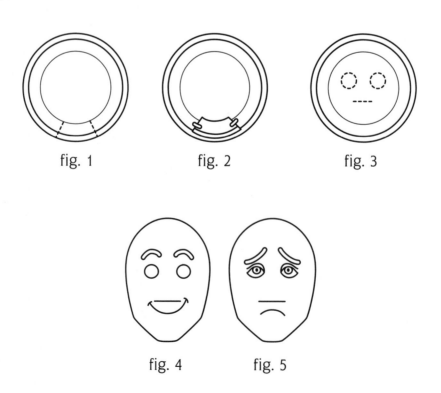

fig. 1   fig. 2   fig. 3

fig. 4   fig. 5

David's Fight with Goliath

1 Samuel 17:32-50

David depended on God to be his strength when he conquered the giant with a sling and a stone. Encourage children to trust God to be with them and to help them in every situation.

Memory Verse

David said to the Philistine, "You come against me with sword and spear and javelin, but I come against you in the name of the Lord Almighty."

1 Samuel 17:45

Materials

- Two dinner-size paper plates
- Ruler
- Pencil
- Crayons, markers, or paints
- Construction paper (white)
- Scissors
- Glue
- Brass paper fastener

Rotate the back plate to show David's stone sailing toward Goliath.

Suggested Uses

1. As children tell the story in their own words, have them rotate the back plate when they reach the part where David uses his sling to defeat the giant.

2. Have children discuss what special abilities God gave each of them. How can they use their special gifts to serve God?

Directions

1. Color the lower one-third of a dinner-size plate (eating side) to resemble the ground. Color the rest of the plate to resemble the sky.

2. Copy the David and Goliath patterns on page 39. Cut out and color the patterns.

3. Glue the figures of David and Goliath across from each other on the plate, leaving at least 3.5" (9 cm) of space between them.

4. Use a pencil to draw a curved section about 1" (2.5 cm) wide between David's sling and Goliath's head (fig. 1).

5. Carefully cut out the curved section (fig. 2).

6. Color the eating side of a second paper plate to resemble the sky.

7. Put the plate with David and Goliath on top of the second plate. Attach the plates at their centers with a brass paper fastener.

8. Draw a stone inside the cutout section so that when the back plate is turned, the stone travels from David's sling to Goliath's head (fig. 3).

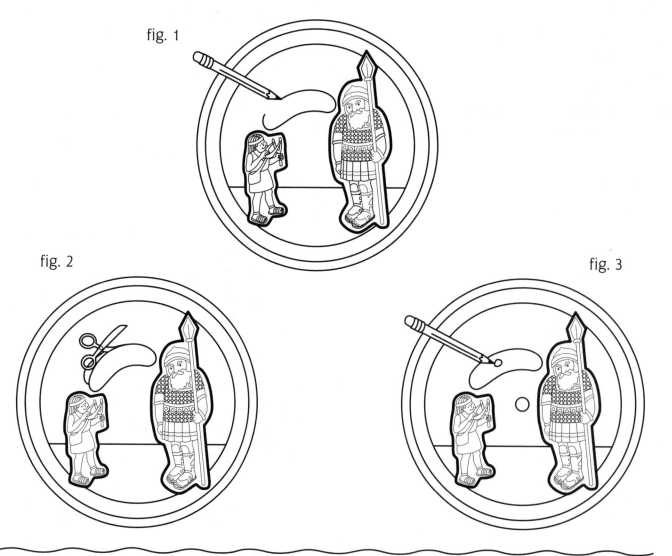

fig. 1

fig. 2

fig. 3

David's Fight with Goliath Patterns

Elijah Fed by Ravens

Toss and Catch Game

1 Kings 16:30-34; 17:1-6

Help the raven get God's gift of food into Elijah's mouth.

Suggested Uses

1. Have children take turns playing the game and keeping score.

2. Have children discuss other times when God gave gifts of food to His people.

The prophet Elijah said that there would be no rain in Israel except at his word for a few years because of King Ahab's evil actions. God told Elijah to hide from King Ahab by a brook. Elijah drank water from the brook and God sent ravens to feed him.

Memory Verse

"You will drink from the brook, and I have ordered the ravens to feed you there."

1 Kings 17:4

Materials

- Two sturdy paper bowls
- Pencil
- Scissors
- Glue
- Jumbo craft stick
- Crayons, markers, or paints
- Two tiny plastic wiggle eyes for raven (optional)
- Two large plastic wiggle eyes for Elijah (optional)
- Yarn
- Stiff cardboard
- Ruler
- String
- Paper hole punch

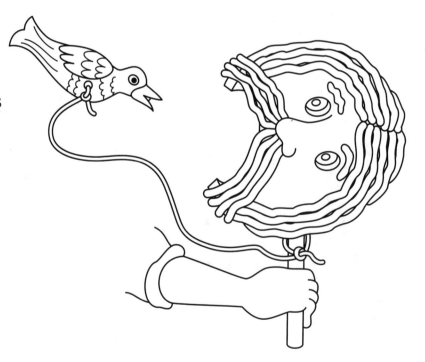

Directions

1. Cut a paper bowl as shown (fig. 1).

2. Duplicate this cut bowl exactly by putting the cutout bowl inside a second bowl and using a pencil to trace along the cut edge. Remove the bowl and cut along the traced line to make the bowls the same shape.

3. Glue a jumbo craft stick to the rim of one of the bowls to make a handle (fig. 2).

4. Glue the two bowls together rim-to-rim (eating sides facing inward) to form an opening to make Elijah's opened mouth (fig. 3).

5. Color a nose and eyes or glue on large plastic wiggle eyes.

6. Cut pieces of yarn and glue them to the head for hair and a mustache.

7. Copy and cut two copies of the raven pattern on page 41. Glue one copy to heavy cardboard. Cut out. Glue the other copy to the other side of the cardboard.

8. Color both sides of the raven black and the piece of meat in the raven's beak red. Color eyes or glue tiny plastic wiggle eyes on the raven.

9. Use a paper hole punch to make a small hole in the raven where the pattern indicates. Tie one end of a 20" (50 cm) piece of string through the hole. Tie the other end of the string to the jumbo craft stick. Secure with a spot on glue on the knot.

10. To play, hold the handle in one hand and swing the raven into Elijah's mouth.

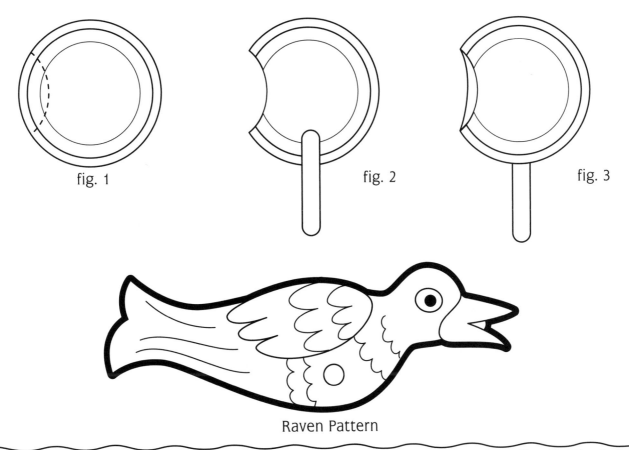

fig. 1   fig. 2   fig. 3

Raven Pattern

God Cares for You

Turn the wheel of emotions to see that God cares for you at all times.

Suggested Uses

1. Have children remember an incident when they were happy, angry, sad, worried, or frightened, and turn the wheel to that face. Then, have them describe in pictures or words what happened and how God cared for them.

2. Have children repeat the memory verse together.

Materials

- Two dinner-size paper plates
- Scissors
- Pencil
- Crayons, markers, or paints

Having faith in God means relying more on Him than on our own emotions. Even when we are tempted to feel sad or worried, we can have comfort and strength knowing that the Lord cares for us. He is ready to protect us and strengthen us in any situation.

Memory Verse

God is our refuge and strength, an ever-present help in trouble.

Psalms 46:1

Directions

1. Using the bottom of a cup or another small, round object, draw two 2" (5 cm) diameter circles opposite each other on the eating side of a dinner-size plate. Cut out just the top circle (fig. 1).

2. Color a face with a big smile in the other circle. Write the words "If you feel" "Smile" and "God cares for you!" on the plate. (See finished craft on page 42.)

3. Put the plate with the smiling face inside another dinner-size paper plate and attach the plates at their centers with a brass paper fastener. (See page 6 for instructions for finding the exact center of a plate.) Then, turn the back plate and trace the cutout circle on each quarter section of the back plate to make four circles (fig. 2).

4. Remove the brass paper fastener and draw or color a face on each of the circles to show a different emotion. See fig. 3 for emotion examples. Be sure to draw the faces so that they are oriented correctly when the top plate is turned.

5. Rejoin the plates with the brass paper fastener so that the back plate can be turned to show each of the faces.

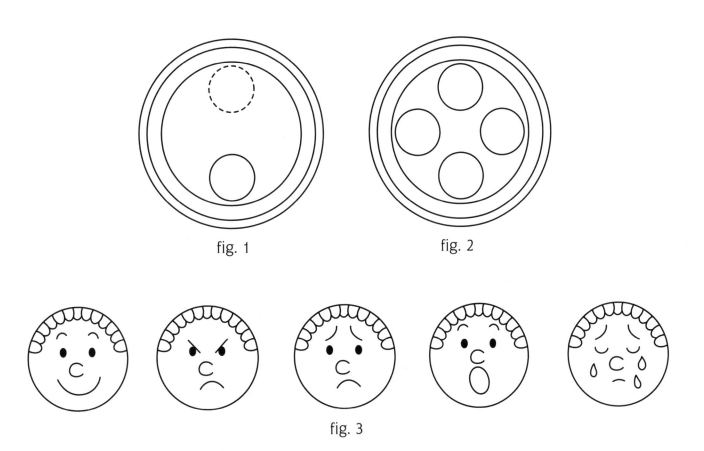

fig. 1   fig. 2

fig. 3

Guardian Angel

Hang this angel on a doorknob as a reminder that God sends angels to watch over us.

Suggested Uses

1. Children can give the angels as gifts to friends and relatives to remind them that God sends angels to minister to us.

2. Create a Christmas display depicting the multitude of angels that appeared to the shepherds.

Materials

- Two dinner-size paper plates
- One dessert-size paper plate
- Pencil
- Scissors
- Glue
- Crayons, markers, or paints
- Glitter (optional)

Hebrews 1:14 tells us that angels are ministering spirits sent to serve believers. Psalm 103:20 tells us that angels obey the voice of God's word. When we speak God's word over our circumstances, it gives our angels something to do. Encourage children to keep their angels busy by speaking God's word about issues in their lives. Children can start by personalizing the memory verse: "Thank you, God, for commanding angels to guard me in all my ways."

Memory Verse

He will command His angels concerning you to guard you in all your ways.

Psalm 91:11

Directions

1. Draw the angel's robe on a dinner-size plate and cut out along the lines (fig. 1).

2. Draw the angel's head and wings on a second dinner-size plate and cut out (fig. 2).

3. Glue the head to the robe and a wing to each side of the robe. (See finished craft above.)

4. Color the angel and add facial features, hair, sleeves, and hands.

5. Add sparkle to the robe and wings by sprinkling wet glue with glitter. Let dry.

6. To make a hanger, cut out the center of a dessert-size plate. (Don't cut through the rim.)

7. Write the words, "An Angel to Watch Over Me" around the hanger, leaving space at the bottom.

8. Glue the hanger to the back of the angel's head.

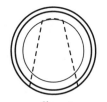

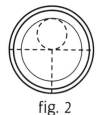

fig. 1   fig. 2

God Cares for His Animals

Psalms 104:10–28

God cares for all of His creatures. He provides food, water, shelter, and every thing that they need. After reading Psalms 104:10–28, ask children to think of ways that their heavenly Father cares for their needs.

Memory Verse

How many are your works, O Lord! In wisdom you made them all; the earth is full of your creatures.

Psalm 104:24

Materials

- One sturdy dinner-size paper plate
- One sturdy dessert-size paper plate
- Crayons, markers, or paints
- Ruler
- Pencil
- Scissors
- Glue
- Construction paper (variety of colors)
- Poster board (white)
- Brass paper fasteners
- Paper hole punch
- Ribbon or yarn

Wall Pockets

Hang the animal pockets on a wall as a reminder that God loves and cares for all of His creations.

Suggested Uses

1. Have children use the animal pockets to hold mail, mementos, or Bible verses to memorize.

2. Have children discuss what they can do to protect God's creatures. If they have pets, how do they care for them?

Optional Materials

Eyes: plastic wiggle eyes, buttons, beads, foam balls, egg carton sections, bottle caps

Nose: folded construction paper for three-dimensional effect, thread spool, cork, small paper cup, bottle cap, pompon, small paper cone, section cut from cardboard tube

Legs: yarn, accordion folded strips of construction paper, chenille craft sticks

Trunk: paper plate rim

Hair: yarn, string, curled gift-wrap ribbon, steel wool, unraveled rope, fluffed-out cotton balls, fringed construction paper

Fur: craft fur

Mane: loops of yarn, fringe, raffia, curled narrow strips of construction paper, curled gift-wrap ribbon, strips of corrugated cardboard

Tail: yarn, narrow spiral paper strip, twine, paper plate rim, chenille craft stick

Fleece: cotton balls, plastic foam packing pieces, white tissue paper crumbled into balls, curled pieces of white yarn

Feathers: craft feathers, sections of paper plate rims

Directions

1. To make the wall pocket, color the bottom of a sturdy dinner-size paper plate. Cut the plate in half. Glue the two halves together, rim-to-rim (with the eating sides facing inward), to form a pocket.

2. Choose an animal to decorate the front of the pocket. (See the illustrations below for ideas.) To make the animal, color or paint the bottom of a dessert-size paper plate to resemble the chosen animal.

3. Cut any movable parts such as wings, ears, and tails from poster board. Attach the parts with brass paper fasteners.

4. Color facial features and other details onto the animal or glue on any of the optional materials.

5. Glue the animal to the front of the pocket. Use a paper hole punch to make a hole at each end of the pocket. Tie a length of ribbon or yarn through the holes to hang.

Praise God

Psalm 150

Encourage children to jump, shout, sing, and praise God for the things He has done and the wonderful gifts He has given.

Memory Verse

Praise him with tambourine and dancing.

Psalms 150:4

Materials

- Two sturdy dinner-size paper plates
- Glue
- Crayons, markers, or paints
- Pencil
- Ruler
- Paper hole punch
- Small bells
- Ribbon

Tambourine

Sing and use the tambourine to praise God with music!

Suggested Uses

1. Have children write songs praising God, then sing the songs while shaking their tambourines.

2. Have children reenact Miriam's celebration after crossing the Red Sea. (Exodus 15:19–21)

Directions

1. Glue two sturdy dinner-size plates together, rim-to-rim, (with the eating sides facing inward).

2. Write "Praise God" around the edge of the tambourine. Decorate the plates.

3. Use a paper hole punch to make evenly spaced holes around the edge of the tambourine. Tie a bell at each hole with a piece of ribbon, leaving the ends of the ribbon long.

Peacemakers

Lion and Lamb Caddies

The lion and lamb caddies remind children of the peace that God desires for all of us.

Suggested Uses

1. Use the animals to hold desk supplies.

2. Fill the animals with treats or other party favors for a table decoration.

3. Tell the story of Noah and the ark.

When God restores the earth, the lion and the lamb will live in peace and little children will play with them! This is the kind of peace that we can look forward to. Encourage children to be peacemakers on Earth until then.

Memory Verse

The wolf will live with the lamb, the leopard will lie down with the goat, the calf and the lion and the yearling together; and a little child will lead them.

Isaiah 11:6

Materials

- Sturdy paper bowls (two for each animal)
- Ruler
- Pencil
- Scissors
- Stiff cardboard (white)
- Construction paper (black)
- Glue
- Crayons, markers, or paint
- Yarn (for lion)
- Cotton balls (for lamb)

Directions

Lion

1. Copy the lion head, leg, and tail patterns on page 50. Glue the patterns onto stiff cardboard and cut out. Make four legs.

2. Follow steps 2–6 for the lamb.

3. Color both sides of the lion. Use yarn for the lion's mane.

Lamb

1. Copy the lamb head, leg, ear, and tail patterns on page 50. Glue the patterns onto stiff cardboard and cut out. Make four legs and two ears.

2. Cut away the top third of a sturdy paper bowl (fig. 1).

3. Place the cutout bowl inside a second sturdy paper bowl and use a pencil to trace along the cut edge. Remove the cutout bowl and cut along the traced line.

4. Glue the head and tail onto the rim of one bowl (fig. 2).

5. Glue the bowls together, rim-to-rim (eating sides facing inward), to form a pocket.

6. Glue the legs on each side of the body. The feet should rest evenly on a flat surface.

7. Fold the ears. Use glue to attach one ear to each side of the head.

8. Color both sides of the lamb. Use cotton balls for the lamb's wool.

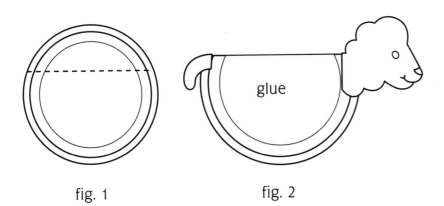

fig. 1   fig. 2

Peacemakers Patterns

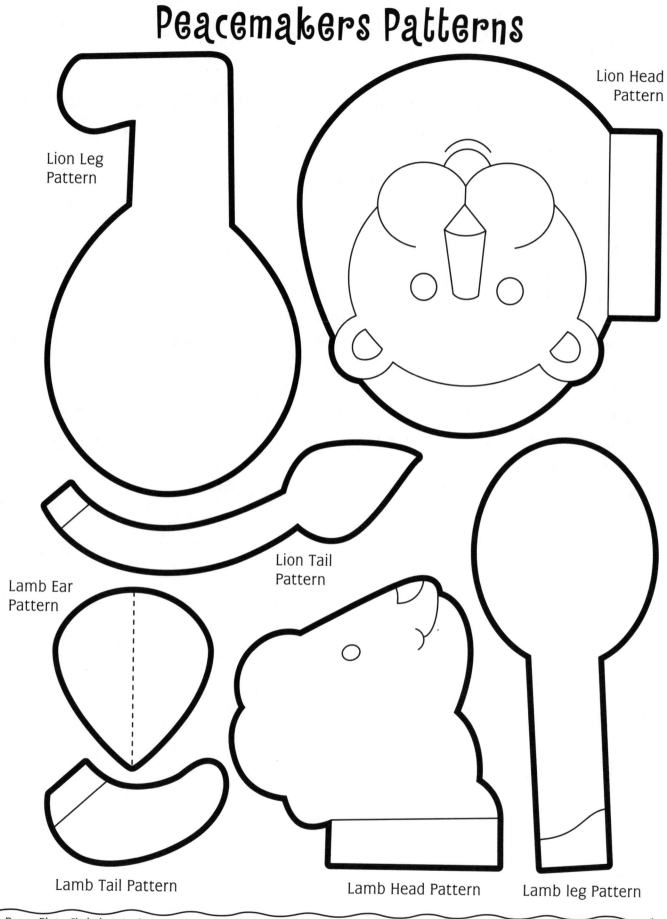

Lion Head Pattern

Lion Leg Pattern

Lion Tail Pattern

Lamb Ear Pattern

Lamb Tail Pattern

Lamb Head Pattern

Lamb leg Pattern

Three Men in a Fiery Furnace

Daniel 3:4-29

Shadrach, Meshach, and Abednego refused to worship any god other than the Most High God. They trusted in God, and He saved them from a fiery furnace—and even from smelling like smoke!

Memory Verse

"They trusted in Him . . . and were willing to give up their lives rather than serve or worship any god except their own God."

Daniel 3:28

Materials

- One sturdy dinner-size paper plate
- Scissors
- Ruler
- Pencil
- Poster board (white)
- Construction paper (gray and white)
- Glue
- Crayons, markers, or paints

Pull-Tab Toy

Open the door to the fiery furnace to see that God kept the three men from harm.

Suggested Uses

1. Have children repeat these words of Shadrach, Meshach, and Abednego each time they open the furnace door: "The God we serve is able to save us."

2. Let children tell the story in their own words as they play with the toy.

Directions

1. Cut a sturdy dinner-size plate as shown (fig. 1).

2. Use a pencil and a ruler to draw two 0.75" (2 cm) vertical lines on the eating side of the plate 4" (10 cm) apart. Cut slits along the lines. Mark the slits *A* and *B* (fig. 2).

3. Cut a 0.75" x 8" (2 cm x 20 cm) strip from poster board. Fold the strip upward 1.5" (4 cm) from the end, then unfold it (fig. 3).

4. Cut a 1.5" x 0.25" (4 cm x 1 cm) rectangular strip (to serve as a stop tab) from poster board and glue it to the left side of the fold (fig. 4).

5. Turn the plate over and insert the long end of the strip into slot B. Insert the short end of the strip into slot A (fig. 5). Turn the plate over. Fold the strip next to the stop tab.

6. To make a door for the furnace, cut a 4" x 8" (10 cm x 20 cm) piece of poster board and fold it in half crosswise (fig. 6). Unfold and cover one (inside) side entirely with glue.

7. Glue the door closed with the A side of the strip between the two halves of the door (fig. 7). Use scissors to round the top corners of the door.

8. Copy and cut out the pattern on page 53. Color the figures and glue them to the center of the plate. Color the furnace, and flames behind the men.

9. Close the door. Pull the tab to see the unharmed men and Jesus inside the fiery furnace.

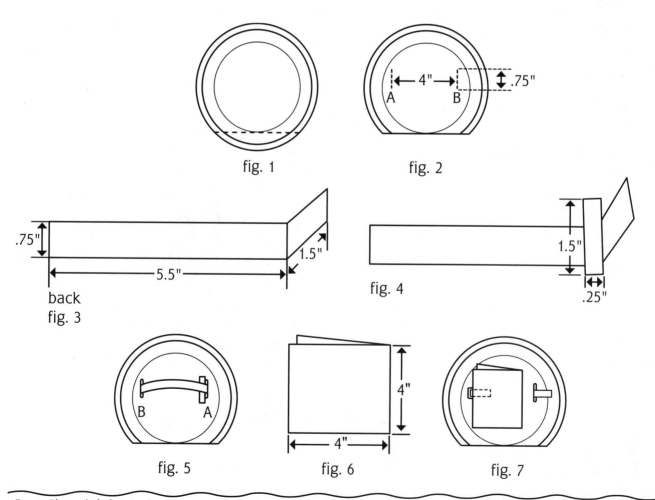

fig. 1 fig. 2

.75" 5.5" 1.5" back fig. 3

1.5" .25" fig. 4

fig. 5 4" 4" fig. 6 fig. 7

Three Men in a Fiery Furnace Pattern

Daniel in the Lions' Den

This puzzle illustrates the story of Daniel in the lions' den.

Suggested Uses

1. Let children exchange their puzzles with friends to assemble.

2. Have children draw their own Bible story pictures. Then, glue them to plates to make puzzles.

Daniel continued to pray to God even after the king made praying to anyone but him illegal. Discuss the meaning of the phrase, "Dare to be a Daniel." (Like Daniel—pray consistently, live a life of integrity, and trust God to take care of you.)

Memory Verse

"My God sent His angel, and he shut the mouths of the lions."

Daniel 6:22

Materials

- Two sturdy dinner-size plates
- Pencil
- Crayons, markers, or paints
- Scissors
- Resealable plastic sandwich bag
- Glue

Directions

1. Copy and cut out the pattern below. Glue the pattern to the eating side of a sturdy dinner-size plate. Color the pattern.

2. On the back of the plate, draw lines to divide the plate into puzzle pieces.

3. Carefully cut out the puzzle pieces.

4. Use another paper plate as a base on which to put together the puzzle. Store the puzzle pieces in a resealable plastic sandwich bag.

Jonah in the Big Fish

Mobile

This mobile illustrates Jonah's rescue by a big fish.

Suggested Uses

1. Display the mobile from a ceiling light fixture or in a doorway.
2. Allow children to tell the story in their own words.

Materials

- Three sturdy dinner-size paper plates
- Pencil
- Ruler
- Scissors
- Poster board (white)
- Glue
- Crayons, markers, or paints
- Two plastic wiggle eyes (optional)
- Sturdy thread
- Paper hole punch
- Yarn

Jonah disobeyed God and boarded a ship for Tarshish instead of going to Nineveh as the Lord had told him to do. The ship sailed into a big storm. When Jonah was thrown overboard, God sent a big fish to rescue him and give him a second chance. When Jonah prayed and praised God, the Lord commanded the fish to spit Jonah onto dry land. Remind children that the place of obedience is always the best place to be!

Memory Verse

"In my distress I called to the Lord, and He answered me."

Jonah 2:2

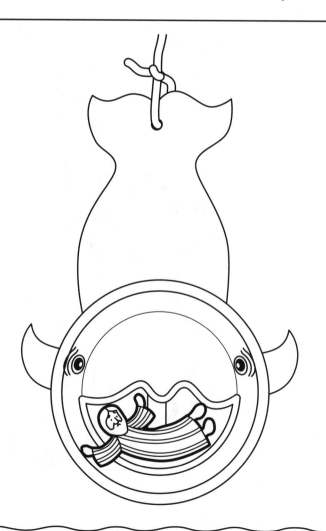

Directions

1. Draw a 6" x 3.5" (15 cm x 9 cm) opened mouth on the non-eating side of a sturdy dinner-size plate (fig. 1). Cut out the opened mouth.

2. Cut a second sturdy dinner-size plate (or poster board) to make the fish's body (fig. 2).

3. Copy the fin pattern on page 58 onto poster board. Trace and cut out two fins.

4. Glue the body and the fins to the rim of the plate with the cutout mouth (fig. 3).

5. Color both sides of the fish gray. Add eyes, or you may prefer to glue on plastic wiggle eyes.

6. Copy the Jonah pattern. Color and cut out.

7. Fold the pattern and glue a piece of poster board between it with the end of a piece of sturdy thread sandwiched between the hands. Cut out.

8. Glue the other end of the thread to the inside of the fish's head so that Jonah can turn freely inside the fish's mouth.

9. Color the eating side of a third sturdy dinner-size plate pink to make the inside of the fish's mouth. Color the rest of the plate gray.

10. Glue the pink side of the plate, rim-to-rim (eating sides facing inward) to the back of the fish's head so that Jonah is enclosed in the fish's pink mouth.

11. Use a paper hole punch to make a hole in the top center of the fish's tail. Tie a piece of yarn from the hole for hanging.

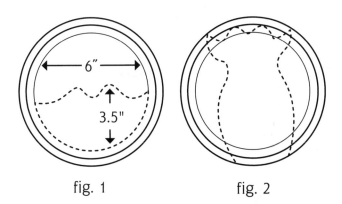

fig. 1   fig. 2

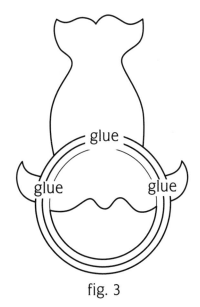

fig. 3

Jonah in the Big Fish Patterns

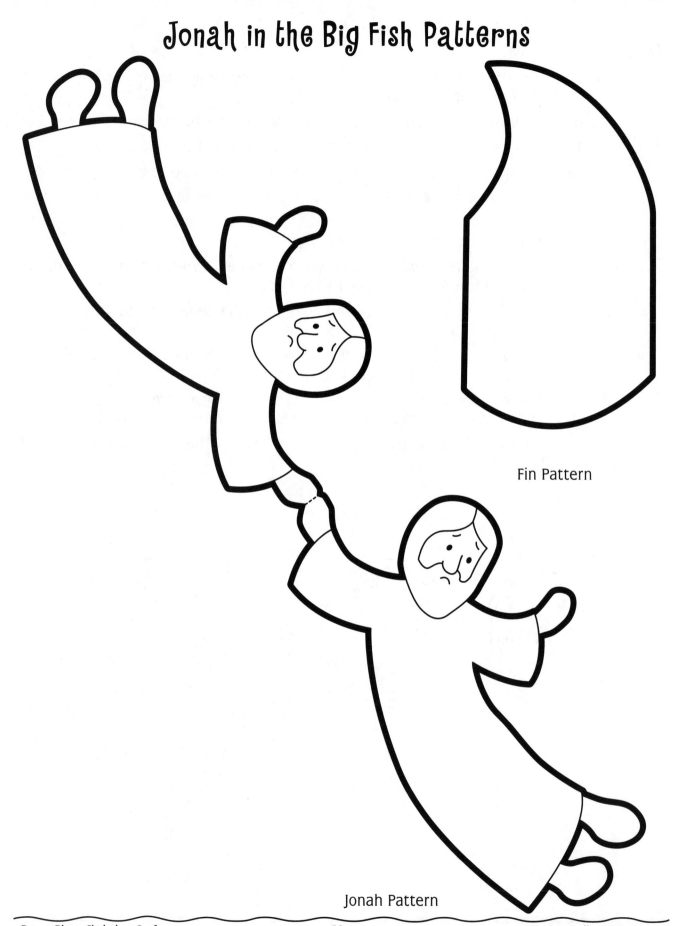

Fin Pattern

Jonah Pattern

Jesus Is Born

Luke 2:1-20; Matthew 2:1-12

Ask children to imagine what it might have been like for shepherds watching their flocks when an angel suddenly appeared to them. Scripture tells us that they were terrified! No wonder the first words the angel spoke were, "Do not be afraid." Rejoice with children that the good news the angels brought is for all people—for Jewish shepherds, for the Gentile Magi, and for us!

Memory Verse

The angel said to them, "Do not be afraid. I bring you good news of great joy that will be for all the people."

Luke 2:10

Materials

- One flexible dinner-size paper plates (One plate makes two 6" (15 cm) figures.)
- Ruler
- Pencil
- Scissors
- Fine-line markers (variety of colors)
- Glue
- Poster board (white)
- Paper clips

Stand-Up Nativity Figures

Celebrate Christmas with these Nativity figures.

Suggested Uses

1. Allow children to arrange the figures to tell the Nativity story.
2. Display the Nativity scene at church or at home as a table centerpiece.

Optional Materials

- Hair and Beards: embroidery floss, string, cotton balls, curled paper, gift-wrap ribbon
- Crowns and Halos: aluminum foil, metallic paper, construction paper
- Angel Robe and Wings: paper doilies, tinsel, glitter
- Magi Robes: foil doilies, metallic rickrack, tinsel, sequins
- Shepherd Staff: pipe cleaner

Directions

1. To make a robe for each Nativity figure, cut a flexible paper plate in half. Decorate one-half of the plate to make a robe. Put the leftover half aside to use for another figure.

2. Overlap the cut edges of the robe to form a cone, leaving a 0.5" (1.25 cm) wide opening at the top. Secure with glue and hold in place with a paper clip until dry (fig. 1). Use scissors to trim the bottom of the cone so that it rests evenly on a flat surface.

3. Copy the patterns on page 61 onto poster board. Add facial features and hair to the head patterns with fine-line markers or glue on one of the optional materials for hair.

4. Put glue on the tab and insert it into the opening at the top of the cone.

5. Color both sides of the arm patterns, then glue the center of the pattern to the back of the cone. Color or glue on optional materials and decorative trims.

6. To make an angel, cut halo and headdress pieces from poster board. Color or glue on the optional materials and decorative trims. Glue the angel's hands together in prayer. Glue the angel's wings to its back.

7. To make Baby Jesus with Mary, color the Baby Jesus pattern and glue it in Mary's arms.

8. To make a shepherd, bend a pipe cleaner to look like a staff and glue to the shepherd's hand. Hold in place with paper clips until dry.

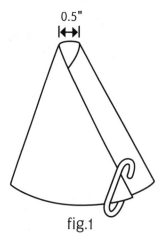

0.5"

fig.1

Jesus Is Born Patterns

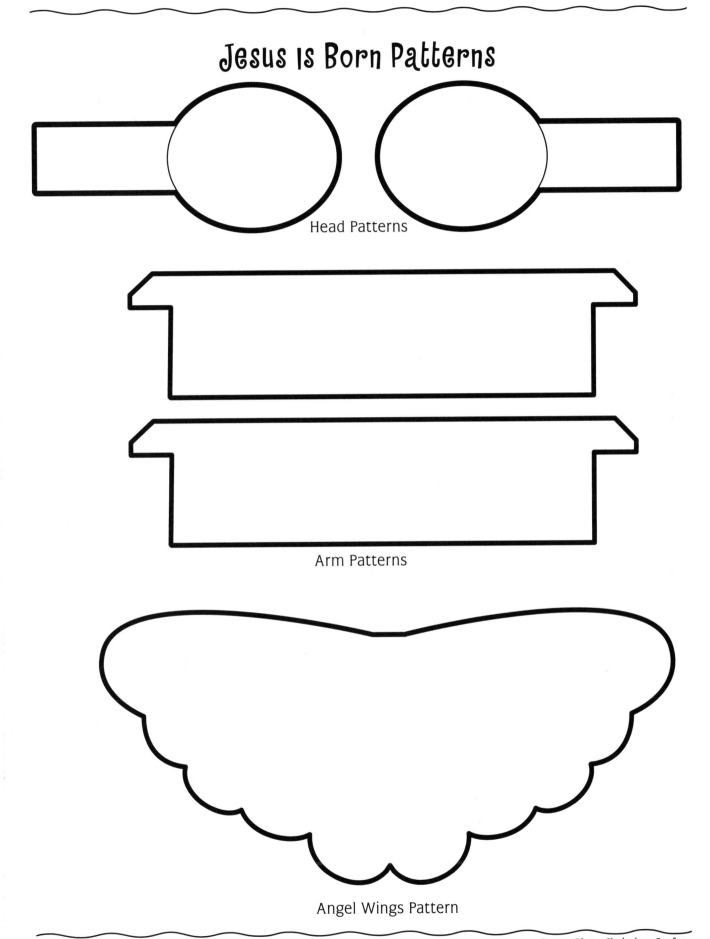

Head Patterns

Arm Patterns

Angel Wings Pattern

Happy Birthday, Jesus

Pretend Cake

Luke 1:26-38

Rotate the back plate to "light" the candles on Jesus' birthday cake.

Suggested Uses

1. Light the candles on the cake and sing "Happy Birthday" to Jesus.

2. Have children say special prayers to Jesus as gifts at His birthday party celebration.

Materials

- Two dinner-size paper plates
- Pencil
- Scissors
- Crayons, markers, or paints
- Brass paper fastener

God chose Mary to be the mother of His son, Jesus. As you celebrate His birthday, thank God for giving us the gift of His son.

Memory Verse

The angel said to her . . . "You will be with child and give birth to a son, and you are to give him the name Jesus."

Luke 1:30–31

Directions

1. Put one dinner-size plate inside a second dinner-size plate and punch a hole through their centers.

2. Copy and cut out the cake pattern below. Glue the pattern to the bottom half of the eating side of one plate.

3. Copy and cut out the candle pattern below. Trace the pattern onto the plate to make three candles on the cake.

4. Cut out the three flame shapes from the plate (fig. 1).

5. Color the cake.

6. Around the rim of the plate, write "Happy Birthday, Jesus."

7. Color one-half of the other plate's eating side bright orange, then put the plate with the cake inside the orange plate.

8. Insert a brass paper fastener though the hole in the centers of the plates.

9. "Light" the candles by rotating the back plate.

fig. 1

Magi Follow the Star

Rotate the back plate to watch the Magi follow the star to find the child Jesus.

Suggested Uses

1. Have children tell the story in their own words as they play with the toy.

2. Have children say the memory verse as they turn the wheel.

Materials

- Two dinner-size paper plates
- Pencil
- Crayons, markers, or paints
- Scissors
- Ruler
- Glue
- Brass paper fastener

The Magi followed a star that led them to Jesus. When they saw Him, they first worshiped Him and then gave Him very valuable gifts. Inform children that while most manger scenes include the Magi, the Bible teaches that the Magi found Jesus at a house when He was a child (probably around 18 months old). (The idea that the Magi were at the manger came from a desire to create one image that would illustrate all of the stories related to the birth and early years of Jesus.)

Memory Verse

"We saw his star in the east and have come to worship him."

Matthew 2:2

Directions

1. Copy and cut out the patterns on page 66. Color the figures.

2. Fold a dinner-size plate in half to find the center. Cut the plate into two pieces about 0.5" (1.25 cm) off center so that one piece is bigger than the other (fig. 1). Discard the smaller piece.

3. Color the eating side of the larger piece brown to resemble the ground and glue the figures of the Magi pattern onto the plate piece (fig. 2).

4. Put the plate piece inside a second plate and draw a line across the cut edge.

5. Remove the plate with the Magi and color the smaller section above the line to resemble the ground and the larger section to resemble sky. Draw a large star near the top.

6. Copy and cut out the Jesus' family pattern on page 66. Glue the Jesus' family pattern onto the ground section of the plate (fig. 3).

7. Align the Magi plate piece with the line drawn across the other plate. Attach the plates with a brass paper fastener.

8. Turn the back plate to change the scene from the Magi following the star to the Magi finding the child.

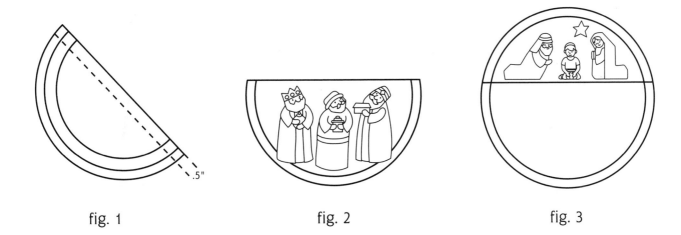

fig. 1   fig. 2   fig. 3

Magi Follow the Star Patterns

Gifts of the Magi

Matthew 2:9-12

This decoration contains fragrant potpourri to remind children of the gifts brought by the Magi.

Suggested Uses

1. Hang the decorations in closets to perfume clothes.
2. Give the decorations as Christmas gifts.

Materials

- Two dessert-size paper plates
- Potpourri
- Scissors
- Pictures related to Jesus' birth
- Glue
- Paper hole punch
- Yarn or string

Matthew 2:9–12

Read Matthew 2:11 and remind children that the first gift the Magi presented to Jesus was worship. Then, they presented gifts of gold, incense, and myrrh. Remind children that God wants our hearts first, then our gifts.

Memory Verse

They bowed down and worshiped him. Then they opened their treasures and presented him with gifts of gold and of incense and of myrrh.

Matthew 2:11

Directions

1. On the non-eating side of a dessert-size plate, glue a picture that relates to Jesus' birth.
2. Around the rim of the plate, write "Jesus the Savior Is Born."
3. Turn the plate over and put potpourri onto the eating side of the plate.
4. On a second plate, use a paper hole punch to make holes around the plate about 0.75" (2 cm) from the edge and about 2" (5 cm) apart. The holes will allow the scent to escape.
5. Glue the plate rim-to-rim (eating sides facing inward) to the plate containing the potpourri (fig. 1).
6. Punch a hole at the top of the plates. Tie a loop of yarn through the hole for hanging.

fig. 1

Jesus' Baptism

Flying Dove

This toy dove symbolizes the Holy Spirit descending upon Jesus like a dove.

Suggested Uses

1. Have children make their doves' wings flap as they show how the Holy Spirit descended like a dove at Jesus' baptism.

2. Have children use the dove to tell the story of Noah's ark. (Genesis 6–9)

John at first objected to baptizing Jesus, but then he obeyed. Jesus humbled himself to be baptized by John as an example for us to follow. His baptism was a big deal in Heaven and on the earth. Like any special event, the whole family showed up. The Holy Spirit descended on Jesus like a dove and the Father spoke, "This is my Son, whom I love; with him I am well pleased."

Memory Verse

Jesus replied, "Let it be so now; it is proper for us to do this to fulfill all righteousness."

Matthew 3:15

Materials

- One sturdy dinner-size paper plate
- Three sturdy dessert-size paper plates
- Poster board (white)
- Pencil
- Scissors
- Paper hole punch
- Glue
- Two brass paper fasteners
- Crayons, markers, or paints
- Two small plastic wiggle eyes (optional)
- Construction paper for beak (optional)
- Yarn or string
- Bead (optional)

Directions

1. Copy and cut out the dove head pattern on page 70. Glue the pattern onto a piece of poster board.

2. Trace the dove's body pattern on page 70 onto a sturdy dinner-size plate. Cut out the body shape and use a paper hole punch to make two holes where the pattern indicates.

3. Glue the head to the back of the body (fig. 1).

4. Cut two other dessert-size plates in half to make four wing shapes. (Two wing shapes are needed for each wing.)

5. Hold two of the wing shapes rim to rim, with eating sides facing inward. Use a paper hole punch to make a hole at the top corner of the wing (fig. 2). Do the same with the other pair of wing shapes, turning them so that the wings are mirrored (fig. 3).

6. Attach the wings to the body with brass paper fasteners.

7. Pull each wing out to the side and glue the two wing shapes together with a dab of glue at each bottom corner (fig. 3).

8. Color eyes and a beak on the dove's head, or glue on plastic wiggle eyes and make a beak. To make a double beak, fold a small piece of construction paper in half and cut a triangle with the base of the triangle on the fold (fig. 4). Glue the bottom part of the beak in place on the head, leaving the top part to pop up.

9. Use a paper hole punch to make a hole at the top of each wing (fig. 5). Thread a 20" (50 cm) string through these holes. Close the wings and tie a knot so that the string is taut but not tight. Leave one end of the string hanging past the dove's tail (fig. 5).

10. To make it easier to pull the string, thread a bead onto the end of the string and secure it with a knot.

11. Hold the dove by the top of its head and with the other hand, pull gently on the string to make the dove's wings flap.

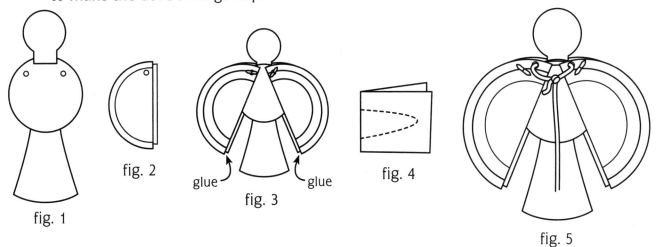

fig. 1

fig. 2

glue   glue

fig. 3

fig. 4

fig. 5

Jesus' Baptism Patterns

Dove Head

Dove Body

The First Disciples

Matthew 4:18-22

Jesus' first disciples were fishermen. They left their nets and their boats to follow Jesus. Jesus' promise to the disciples also applies to us today: as we follow Him, we will "catch" people for His kingdom.

Memory Verse

At once they left their nets and followed him.

Matthew 4:20

Materials

- One paper bowl (Use a plastic bowl if the boat will be floated in water.)
- One dessert-size paper plate
- Small block of foam or play clay
- Glue
- Two plastic drinking straws
- Pencil
- Ruler
- Scissors
- Poster board (white) or paper plate scraps
- Crayons
- Two chenille craft sticks
- Plastic mesh used for packaging fruits and vegetables or nylon netting
- Paper hole punch
- String

Fishing Boat

This toy boat flies the Christian flag, and can really float!

Suggested Uses

1. Allow children to discuss the ways in which they can follow Jesus.

2. Have children repeat the memory verse together.

Directions

1. Glue a small block of foam or attach a small amount of play clay to the center of the bowl. To make a mast, insert one straw partially inside another straw. Glue this mast into the foam or insert into the play clay.

2. Cut a dessert-size plate in half. Glue one-half of the plate to the mast for a sail.

3. Cut a flag from poster board or paper plate scrap. Color a red cross on a blue field in the upper left corner for a Christian flag. Cut a slit in the top of the mast and insert the flag.

4. Copy the fisherman patterns below. Color and cut out.

5. To make a support for the fisherman pattern, bend a chenille craft stick in half and twist it to make a fisherman's head and neck (fig. 1).

6. Thread another craft stick through the twist to make arms. Twist the first stem a few more times to secure the arms and to make a torso. Snip off the ends of the arms and legs to correct proportions. Bend the ends of the arms and legs to make hands and feet (fig. 2).

7. Glue the front and back of the fisherman pattern to each side of the chenille stick support (fig. 3). Fasten the fisherman to the mast.

8. Glue a piece of nylon netting or plastic mesh inside the boat for the fisherman's net.

9. Use a paper hole punch to make a hole in the rim of the bowl. Tie a string through the hole before placing the boat in water so that it doesn't float away.

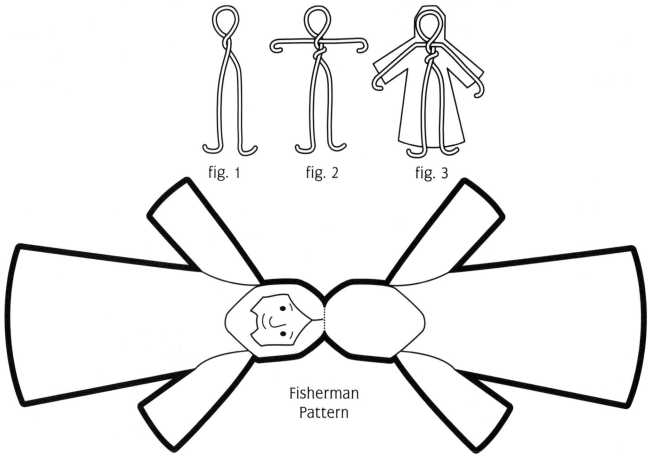

fig. 1   fig. 2   fig. 3

Fisherman
Pattern

Fishers of Men

Mark 1:16-20

Four of Jesus' disciples were fishermen who left their boats and nets to follow Him and teach God's Word. Jesus calls us all to be fishers of people.

Memory Verse

"Come, follow me," Jesus said, "and I will make you fishers of men."

Mark 1:17

Materials

- One sturdy dinner-size plate or platter
- One flexible dinner-size plate (one for each player)
- Pencil
- Scissors
- Stapler
- Construction paper (light colors)
- Paper clips (one for each fish)
- Glue or tape
- Crayons, markers, or paints
- Unsharpened pencils (one for each player)
- String
- Small magnets (one for each player)

Magnetic Fishing Game

This game uses magnets to fish for messages of faith.

Suggested Uses

1. Have children take turns using their fishing poles to catch as many fish as they can. After all of the fish are caught, players read aloud the messages on their fish. The player who catches the most fish is the winner.

2. Write the name of a Bible character on each fish. When a child catches a fish, have her tell something about that person's story. If she does not know anything about that character, have her throw the fish back into the water.

3. Have children repeat the memory verse each time they catch a fish.

Directions

1. Each player will hold his caught fish in a basket. To make a basket, cut four equally-spaced 2.5" (6 cm) triangles around a flexible dinner-size plate (fig. 1). Then, overlap the cut edges and staple (fig. 2).

2. Trace the fish pattern below onto construction paper. Make a front and back for each fish. Ten to fifteen fish are needed to play the game.

3. Glue or tape a paper clip lengthwise on one fish half. A small loop should hang from the mouth (fig. 3). Glue the other fish half over the paper clip. Repeat for each fish.

4. Color one side of each fish. On the other side, write messages such as:

Jesus Is the Way	*Jesus Loves Me*	*Love Your Neighbor*
God Answers Prayer	*God Cares for Me*	*Trust In Jesus*
God Is Love	*Praise God*	*God Is Good*

5. To make a fishing pole and line, glue a magnet to one end of a piece of string. Tie the other end of the string to an unsharpened pencil.

6. Color the eating side of a sturdy paper dinner plate or platter to resemble the sea. Fill the sea with the fish.

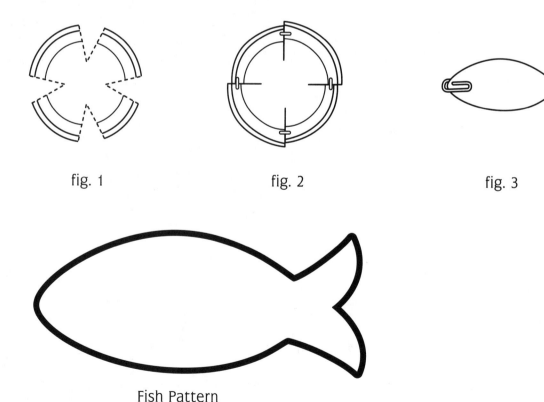

fig. 1   fig. 2   fig. 3

Fish Pattern

God Loves the World

The cross medallion is a reminder of Jesus' death on the cross and His sacrifice for us. Encourage children to wear their medallions with thankfulness for God's love.

Memory Verse

"For God so loved the world that He gave his one and only son, that whoever believes in him shall not perish but have eternal life."

John 3:16

Medallion

Wear this cross medallion to proclaim the good news of Jesus Christ!

Suggested Uses

1. Allow each child to make a medallion to wear or display.

2. Use the medallions to award attendance or Bible memorization.

Materials

- One dessert-size paper plate
- Pencil
- Crayons, markers, or paints
- Glue
- Ribbon
- Stapler

Optional Trim Materials

- Sequins
- Beads
- Metallic rickrack, braid, or cord
- Tinsel
- Glitter
- Foil doilies

Directions

1. Draw a cross in the center of a dessert-size plate (eating side) and write "God Is Love" around the rim.

2. Color the cross and the rest of the plate with decorative designs. If desired, glue on some of the optional trims.

3. Staple the ends of a length of ribbon to the back of the plate to use the medallion as a necklace.

Shine for Jesus

Wall Plaque

This sunny wall plaque is a reminder to let your light shine for Jesus.

Suggested Uses

1. Have children discuss ways that they can let their light shine for Jesus.

2. Children can give the plaques as gifts to brighten someone's day.

Materials

- Two dinner-size paper plates
- One dessert-size paper plate
- Pencil
- Scissors
- Crayons, markers, or paints
- Glue
- Yarn
- Glitter (optional)

Because the Holy Spirit lives in us, we are God's light in the world. Discuss children's unique gifts and talents and the unique ways that they can express God's grace and goodness to the world.

Memory Verse

"You are the light of the world. . . . Let your light shine before men, that they may see your good deeds and praise your Father in heaven."

Matthew 5:14–16

Directions

1. Make a copy of the pattern on page 77.

2. Trace the outline of the pattern onto a dinner-size paper plate. Cut out the plate.

3. Cut the outer rays from the pattern and trace the new pattern onto another dinner-size plate. Cut out the plate.

4. Cut the outer rays from the pattern again and trace the new pattern onto a dessert-size plate. Copy the facial features if desired.

5. Color each plate a different color (red, orange, or yellow).

6. To decorate further, brush glue in places and then sprinkle on glitter to make the sun shine.

7. Glue the plates together at their centers, keeping the plates graduated in size.

8. Glue looped yarn to the back for hanging.

Shine for Jesus Patterns

God Cares for You

Flowered Hat

This colorful flowered hat is a reminder that God, who dresses the fields with flowers, also cares for our needs.

Suggested Uses

1. Have each child create a flowered hat to celebrate Easter, welcome spring, or give as a gift on Mother's Day.

2. Display the hats with the memory verse as a wall decoration.

Materials

- One sturdy 10" or larger paper plate
- One flexible paper bowl
- Scissors
- Glue
- Crayons, markers, or paints
- Construction paper (variety of colors)
- Stapler
- Ribbon
- Tape

God made our world and filled it with beautiful flowers. He gives the seeds, the ground for them to grow in, the rain to feed them, and the sun for them to blossom. God also gives us His love and His teachings to make our lives blossom.

Memory Verse

See how the lilies of the field grow. . . . I tell you that not even Solomon in all his splendor was dressed like one of these.

Matthew 6:28–29

Optional Trim Materials

Flower centers: paper circles, buttons, pompons, half foam balls, painted bottle caps

Flower seeds: tiny beads, dried seeds, paper seeds made with a paper hole punch

Rickrack: construction paper cut with pinking shears

Ruffles: fluted paper muffin cup liners

Paper gift: wrap bow

Curled gift ribbon

Glitter

Feathers

Directions

1. Turn the plate upside down for the hat's brim. Leave as is or cut a design around the edge to make a fancy brim (fig. 1). Cut a hole in the center of the plate. Make the hole slightly smaller than the opening of the bowl.

2. Glue the paper bowl upside down in the center of the plate.

3. Color the hat and decorate with flowers. To make each flower, copy the flower and leaf patterns below onto construction paper. Cut out. Petals can be curled by wrapping around a pencil. (See the optional trim materials list on page 78 for flower centers and seeds.)

4. Glue the flowers and leaves in a pretty arrangement around the brim. Glue desired trims onto the hat. (See the optional trim materials.)

5. Staple two pieces of ribbon to the inside of the hat, doubling it for strength where the staples will be placed. Staple twice, crisscrossing the two staples for added strength (fig. 2). Cover the sharp points of the staples with tape.

fig. 1

fig. 2

Flower Patterns

Leaf Patterns

79

Paper Plate Christian Crafts

Christian Symbols

Sun Catcher

These sun catchers are reminders that Jesus is the light of the world.

Suggested Uses

1. Have each child make a sun catcher to take home and enjoy.
2. Allow children to make sun catchers and distribute them to residents of a nursing home.

Materials

- Two dinner-size paper plates
- Pencil
- Ruler
- Scissors
- Wax paper
- Construction paper (black)
- Paper towels
- Crayon shavings
- Glitter (optional)
- Iron and ironing board (with adult supervision)
- Paper hole punch
- Yarn

Jesus said that He was the light of the world. He promised that those who follow Him will have the light of life. Encourage children to follow Jesus and let their light shine for Him!

Memory Verse

"I am the light of the world. Whoever follows me will never walk in darkness, but will have the light of life."

John 8:12

Directions

1. Cut out the centers of two dinner-size paper plates leaving 1.5" (4 cm) rims (fig. 1). (Do not cut through the rims.)

2. To make two sheets of wax paper slightly larger than the cut out opening in the plates, use one of the cut out rims for a pattern. Lay the rim on top of the wax paper and trace around the inner edge of the rim with a pencil. Remove the rim and extend the circle diameter by 1" (2.5 cm). Cut out the larger circle (fig. 2).

3. Copy and cut out one of the Christian symbol patterns on page 82. Trace the pattern onto black construction paper. Cut out.

4. Cover an ironing board with layers of paper towels. Place a wax paper circle on the towels.

5. Choose crayon shavings of desired colors and sprinkle the shavings onto the wax paper circle. Sprinkle only a few shavings in each area. Do not sprinkle too many different colors in the same area as the color may become muddy. To add sparkle, sprinkle glitter in areas around the symbol.

6. Cover the shavings with the other wax paper circle.

7. (This step should be completed by an adult.) Place a layer of paper towels on top of the wax paper and gently press the wax paper circles together with a warm iron until the crayon shavings melt (fig. 4). Press the iron down, lift it, and place it down in another place rather than using a back and forth movement.

8. Put glue around the inside rim of one of the paper plates and put the pressed wax paper inside the glued rim. Place the other paper plate rim inside the glued rim (fig. 5).

9. Glue the black construction paper shape in the center of the wax paper circle, on the front of the sun catcher.

10. Use a paper hole punch to make a hole at the top center of the sun catcher. Tie a loop of yarn through the hole for hanging.

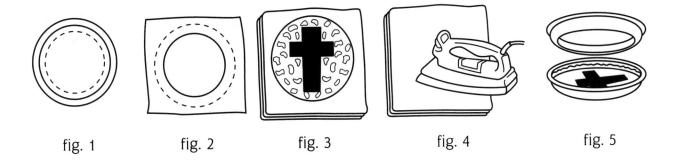

fig. 1   fig. 2   fig. 3   fig. 4   fig. 5

Christian Symbols Patterns

The Good Shepherd

Luke 15:1-7

Tell children that God isn't sitting up in Heaven unconcerned or neutral about whether people are saved or not. He actively seeks them and rejoices (like a shepherd who finds a lost sheep) when they accept Jesus as Lord. The Bible tells us that every time a sinner repents, the angels in Heaven rejoice!

Memory Verse

"Rejoice with me; I have found my lost sheep."

Luke 15:6

Materials

- One sturdy paper plate or platter
- One sturdy dessert-size paper plate
- Pencil
- Scissors
- Ruler
- Crayons, markers, or paints
- Cotton balls
- Glue
- Large paper clip
- Brass paper fastener
- Buttons

Game Board

This game reminds us that Jesus cares for us like a good shepherd cares for his sheep.

Suggested Uses

1. Ask children to imagine what rejoicing in Heaven is like. Have children play the game, then rejoice like those in Heaven do when a lost sheep is found.

2. Make one game for the class, or allow each student to make one to take home or to give as a gift.

Directions

1. Copy and cut out the sheep pattern below. Color the sheep and glue wisps of cotton pulled from a cotton ball to give it a soft, fleecy coat. Glue it to the top edge (eating side) of a sturdy plate or platter.

2. Draw a winding path from a start position at the bottom of the plate to the sheep. Mark the path with squares. Color trees, rocks, bushes, and flowers around the path.

3. To make a spinner, mark the center of a sturdy dessert-size plate's eating side. With a ruler and pencil, draw two straight lines through the center to divide the plate into four equal parts. Number the parts 1–4 (fig. 1).

4. Attach a large paper clip to the center of the dessert-size plate with a brass paper fastener. Keep the fastener a little loose so that the paper clip can spin easily.

5. To play the game, players take turns spinning the paper clip spinner. The number where it stops tells how many spaces they move on the game board. Use buttons for markers. The first player to reach the lost sheep wins.

fig. 1

Sheep Pattern

Prodigal's Pig

Luke 15:11-32

Read the story to children directly from the Bible. Its simple language and story line is accessible even to young children. Explain to children that our heavenly Father is like the father in the story. Even if we go far away, when we return to Him, He runs to us, embraces us, and forgives us.

Memory Verse

"For this son of mine was dead and is alive again; he was lost and is found."

Luke 15:24

Piggy Bank

This piggy bank will remind children of the story of the prodigal son and the time he spent feeding pigs.

Suggested Uses

1. Allow children to take the banks home for personal use.

2. Make a piggy bank for the classroom to collect money for special treats or for an outreach mission.

Materials

- Two sturdy paper cereal bowls
- Ruler
- Pencil
- Poster board (white)
- Scissors
- Glue
- Chenille craft stick
- Plastic soda caps
- Crayons, markers, or paints

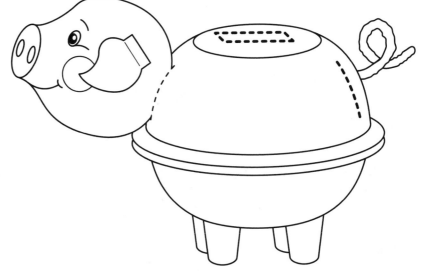

Directions

1. Cut a slot about 0.25" (0.6 cm) wide and 1.5" (4 cm) long in the center of a paper bowl (big enough for a large coin to slip through) and a 1.25" (3.2 cm) slit in the side of the bowl (fig. 1). (This step requires adult supervision.)

2. Copy and cut out the pig's head and ears patterns on page 87. Glue the patterns onto poster board. Cut out.

3. Fold and glue the head parts together, leaving the tabs unglued.

4. Insert the head tabs into the slit at the side of the bowl (fig. 2). Bend the tabs and glue them to the inside of the bowl.

5. Bend the tabs on the ears and glue to the head where the pattern indicates.

6. Poke a small hole in the bowl opposite the head and insert a curled chenille craft stick.

7. Put glue around the rim of the second bowl and join it (eating sides facing inward) to the bowl with the head.

8. Glue four soda caps to the bottom of the pig's belly.

9. Color the pig.

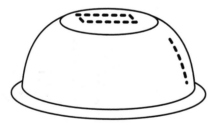

fig. 1

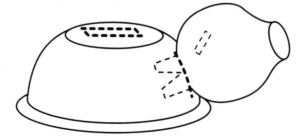

fig. 2

Prodigal's Pig Patterns

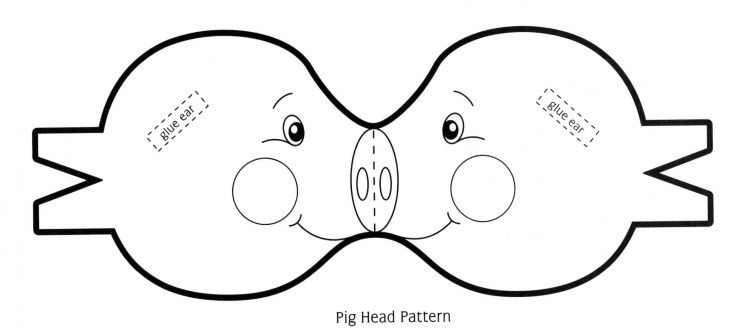

Pig Head Pattern

Pig Ear Patterns

Jesus Loves You This Much!

Give this card to tell someone that Jesus loves and cares for them very much!

Suggested Uses

1. Let each child take his card home. Instruct him to give it to someone who needs to know God's love.

2. Schedule a visit to a nursing home and allow children to give their cards to residents.

Jesus told His disciples to let children come to Him, for the kingdom of Heaven belongs to them. Encourage children to remain childlike in their faith by being quick to believe in God's love and by trusting Him completely. That kind of faith is what living in God's kingdom is all about!

Memory Verse

Jesus said, "Let the little children come to me, and do not hinder them, for the kingdom of Heaven belongs to such as these."

Matthew 19:14

Materials

- One dessert-size paper plate
- Pencil
- Ruler
- Scissors
- Crayons, markers, or paints
- Construction paper
- Glue
- Yarn

closed card

open card

Directions

1. Cut an arched slit 2" (5 cm) wide and 1.5" (3.8 cm) above the edge of a dessert-size paper plate (fig. 1). This slit will be used later to hold the arms in place.

2. Color the back of the plate with a smiling face.

3. Cut two strips from construction paper, each 11" (28 cm) long and 1.5" (3.8 cm) wide.

4. With a ruler and pencil, mark lines on each arm at intervals of 3", 3", 3", and 2" (7.5 cm, 7.5 cm, 7.5 cm, and 5 cm) (fig. 2).

5. Fold each arm using the lines as a guide (fig. 3).

6. Glue each arm to the head, joining the arms beneath the cutout slit (fig. 4).

7. Copy and cut out the hand patterns on page 90. Trace them onto construction paper. Cut out the hands.

8. Glue the hands to the ends of the arms with thumbs facing up.

9. Write "This Much" in the space under the head. (See open card on page 88.)

10. Fold the arms to the center of the head and tuck the thumbs into the slit.

11. Write "Jesus Loves You" on the folded arms. (See closed card on page 88.)

12. Color the greeting card. Use yarn for hair.

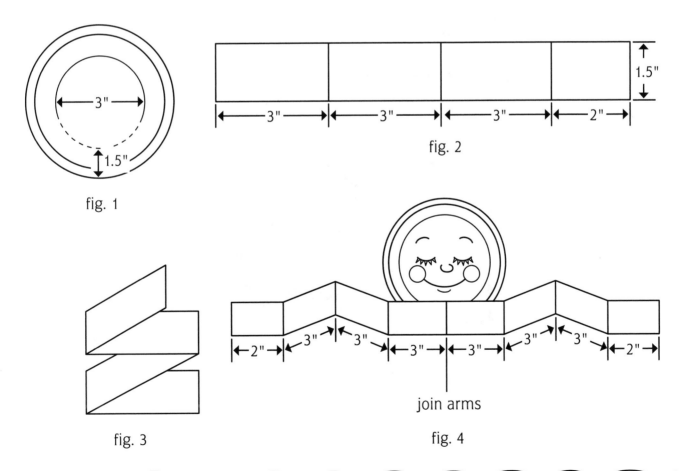

fig. 1

fig. 2

fig. 3

join arms

fig. 4

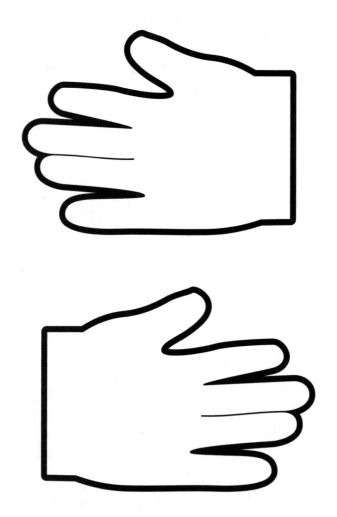

Smile, Jesus Loves You!

Mark 10:13-16

Read the memory verse to children. Invite anyone who has not done so to ask Jesus into her heart and accept Him as her Lord and Savior. Remind children that Jesus won't force His way into our lives. But, He is ready and eager to be invited in.

Memory Verse

"Anyone who will not receive the kingdom of God like a little child will never enter it."

Mark 10:15

Materials

- Two sturdy dinner-size paper plates
- Ruler
- Pencil
- Stiff cardboard
- Scissors
- Glue
- Crayons, markers, or paints
- Balloon, sponge ball, or table tennis ball

Paddle Ball Game

Play the paddle ball game with a friend to send the message that Jesus loves you!

Suggested Uses

1. Have children play the game by marking boundaries and hitting the ball back and forth. The player who fails to hit the ball loses one point to the other player. The first player to ten wins.

2. Have children sing the song "Jesus Loves Me" as they play the paddle ball game.

Directions

1. Cut a handle from stiff cardboard (fig. 1).

2. Glue the handle to the rim of a dinner-size paper plate (fig. 2).

3. Put glue around the rim, including that part of the handle that is glued to the rim. Place a second dinner-size plate on top, rim-to-rim (with the eating sides facing inward) (fig. 3).

4. Color the paddle with a smiley face and write the words "Smile, Jesus Loves You!" around the rim.

5. Use a balloon, sponge ball, or table tennis ball for a ball.

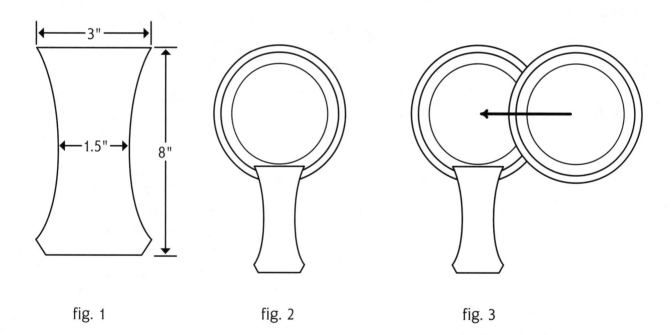

fig. 1   fig. 2   fig. 3

Love Your Neighbor

Mark 12:28-31

When we love God with all of our hearts, souls, and minds, we want to do what pleases Him. Loving our neighbors is a great way to show our love for God. Explain that neighbors include those who look or dress differently than we do, have different customs and beliefs, and even live in different countries.

Memory Verse

"Love your neighbor as yourself."

Mark 12:31

Materials

- One sturdy dinner-size paper plate
- Pencil
- Scissors
- Poster board (white)
- Crayons, markers, or paints
- Glue
- Jumbo craft stick

Use the fan on a warm day to send Jesus' message of love to your neighbors.

Suggested Uses

1. Discuss the work of missionaries in other countries.

2. Attach magnets to the backs of the patterns to make refrigerator magnets.

Directions

1. Choose three of the patterns on page 94 to copy and cut out. Color the patterns and glue them onto poster board.

2. Glue the patterns around the rim of the eating side of a sturdy dinner-size plate.

3. Color a heart on the plate and write the words "Love Your Neighbor" around the rim of the plate.

4. Glue a jumbo craft stick to the back of the plate for a handle.

Love Your Neighbor Patterns

A Net Full of Fish

Luke 5:1–11

The blessings that Jesus gives us are given in abundance! It's God's nature to be openhanded and generous–to pour out more blessings than we have room for! This is what He did for the disciples, and this is what He wants to do for you.

Memory Verse

They caught such a large number of fish that their nets began to break.

Luke 5:6

This plaque shows a net full of fish, one of Jesus' many miracles.

Suggested Uses

1. Have children display the plaques to remind them to tell others about Jesus' miracles.

2. Discuss another time when Jesus filled the disciples' nets with fish. (John 21:1–14)

Materials

- Two dinner-size paper plates
- Pencil
- Crayons
- Watercolor paints
- Paintbrush
- Water
- Scissors
- Plastic netting (used for packaging fruit)
- Glue
- Yarn

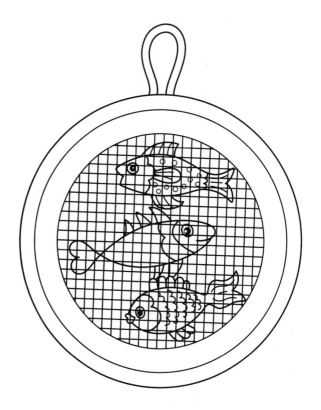

Directions

1. Copy the fish patterns below. Color with wax crayons, pressing firmly so that you get a thick layer of color.

2. Cut out the fish patterns and glue them to the eating side of a dinner-size plate (fig.1).

3. To make a "water" background, sweep a paintbrush dipped in blue watercolor over the plate covering the fish. The wax from the crayons will resist the paint. If too much paint settles in one area, pick it up with a dry, clean brush.

4. Cut the center from a second dinner-size plate so that the rim remains intact.

5. For the fisherman's net, cut a piece from plastic netting. Glue the netting around the inside of the cutout rim (fig. 2).

6. Glue the plate with the netting to the plate with the fish (fig. 3).

7. Glue a loop of yarn to the back of the wall plaque for hanging.

fig. 3

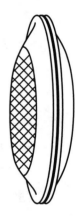

fig. 1

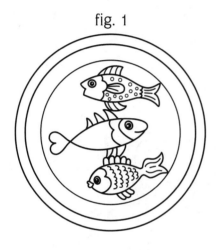

fig. 2

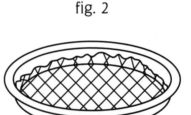

Fish Patterns

Jesus Heals a Paralyzed Man

Luke 5:17-25

This Bible story doesn't tell us much about the faith of the paralyzed man. But, it does tell us that when Jesus saw the faith of the man's friends, He healed the paralyzed man. Encouragè children to pray for their friends.

Memory Verse

"I tell you, get up, take your mat and go home."

Luke 5:24

Materials

- Two sturdy dessert-size paper plates
- One sturdy dinner-size paper plate
- Construction paper (any color)
- Pencil
- Crayons, markers, or paints
- Ruler
- Scissors
- Glue
- Brass paper fastener
- Craft stick

Walking Figure

This toy with moving feet demonstrates what happened when a paralyzed man's friends showed faith in Jesus.

Suggested Uses

1. Have children display the toy to remind them to tell others about Jesus' miracles.

2. Have children repeat the memory verse as they walk the paralyzed man.

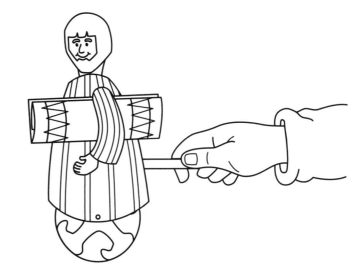

Directions

1. Copy and cut out the head and body patterns on page 98. Glue the head pattern onto a dessert-size plate and the body pattern onto a dinner-size plate. Color and cut out. Glue the head to the back of the body.

2. Copy and cut out the feet pattern on page 98. Glue the feet pattern onto the middle of a second dessert-size plate. Cut out the entire circular shape. Color the feet pattern.

3. Attach the feet to the back of the body with a brass paper fastener.

4. Cut a 2" x 5" (5 cm x 12 cm) piece of construction paper. Decorate the construction paper to make a mat. Cut a slit on each side of the arm and slip the mat through the slits.

5. Glue a craft stick onto the back of the body for a handle. Push while holding the handle to watch the paralyzed man walk after being healed by Jesus.

Jesus Heals a Paralyzed Man Patterns

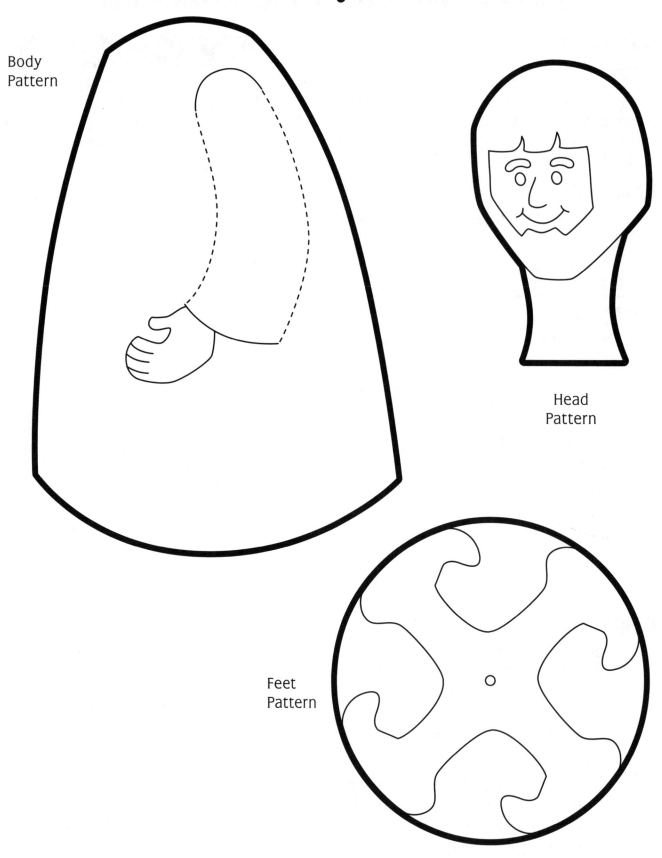

Body
Pattern

Head
Pattern

Feet
Pattern

Jesus Calms the Winds

Matthew 8:23-27

It might seem natural for the disciples to have been afraid in a furious storm, but Jesus rebuked them for their fear and called their faith "little." Jesus spoke to the winds, and they became calm at once. Jesus wants us to be like Him and to speak to the storms in our lives, to always trust Him, and to never be afraid of anything!

Memory Verse

[Jesus] replied, "You of little faith, why are you so afraid?"

Matthew 8:26

Hang the wind sock and watch the streamers blow as a reminder of the miracle Jesus performed when the winds obeyed Him.

Suggested Uses

1. Have children tie their wind socks to tree branches to decorate an area for an outdoor celebration.

2. Have children tie their wind socks to dowel rods or craft sticks and carry them in outdoor processions.

Materials

- One sturdy paper bowl
- Scissors
- Crayons, markers, or paints
- Crepe paper or ribbon
- Tape
- Paper hole punch
- Yarn
- Bells (optional)

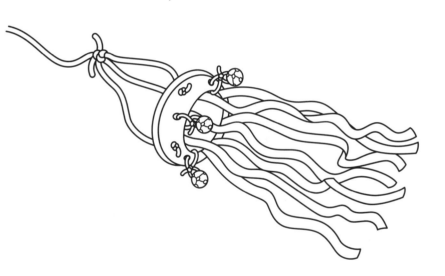

Directions

1. Cut away the bottom of the paper bowl. Do not cut through the rest of the bowl (fig. 1).

2. Color the bowl.

3. Cut 18" (46 cm) streamers from crepe paper or ribbon and glue them around the inside of the bowl. Use a paper hole punch to make holes around the rim of the bowl and attach bells.

4. Use a paper hole punch to make three equally-spaced holes around the bowl. Cut three 12" (30 cm) pieces of yarn and tie a knot at one end of each piece. Thread the other end of each piece through a different hole and tie the pieces together. Tie a longer piece of yarn to the joined pieces for hanging.

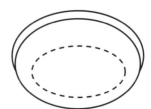

fig. 1

Jairus's Daughter

Stick Puppet

Mark 5:35-42

Close and open the puppet's eyes to show the miracle Jesus performed when he raised Jairus's daughter back to life.

Suggested Uses

1. Have children repeat the memory verse each time they open the puppet's eyes.

2. Allow children to tell the story in their own words as they play with the puppet.

When men brought Jairus the news that his daughter was dead, Jesus ignored them and immediately told Jairus not to fear. Jesus knew that fear and unbelief from Jairus could stop the work He wanted to do. (See Mark 6:5–6.) Encourage children to believe God's Word, act on it without fear, and expect miracles in their lives too!

Memory Verse

Jesus told [Jairus], "Don't be afraid; just believe."

Mark 5:36

Materials

- Two dessert-size paper plates
- Pencil
- Scissors
- Crayons, markers, or paints
- Glue
- Jumbo craft stick
- Brass paper fastener
- Yarn
- Fabric scrap
- Rubber band

Directions

1. Draw two semicircles for eyes on the non-eating side of a dessert-size plate and cut them out (fig. 1).

2. Color the back of the plate a flesh color. Add a mouth, nose, eyebrows, and rosy cheeks (fig. 2). (There are no eyes to add since they are cut out.)

3. Place the plate inside a second dessert-size plate. Use a pencil to trace around the inner edge of the cutout eyes.

4. Remove the plate and color the traced eyes. Then, cut away the rim of the plate and color the rest of the circle a flesh color. Glue a craft stick to the back of the circle (fig. 3).

5. Place the cutout paper circle with the colored eyes inside the plate with the facial features. Line up the cutout eyes with the colored eyes and attach them together with a brass paper fastener (fig. 4).

6. Cut pieces of yarn for hair and glue around the face.

7. Wrap a piece of fabric around the top of the jumbo craft stick. Hold in place with a rubber band to make a dress. Hide the rubber band by folding the fabric over it.

8. Open and close the puppet's eyes by moving the craft stick (figs. 5 and 6).

fig. 1   fig. 2   fig. 3

fig. 4   fig. 5   fig. 6

Jesus Feeds the Hungry People

Pop-Up Toy

This pop-up toy demonstrates Jesus' miracle of feeding over 5,000 people with five loaves of bread and two fish.

Suggested Uses

1. Have children repeat the memory verse each time they push up the stick.

2. Discuss what your church can do to feed hungry people today.

Materials

- Three dinner-size paper plates
- One dessert-size paper plate
- Pencil
- Scissors
- Glue
- Paper clips
- Crayons, markers, or paints
- Jumbo craft stick

Jesus gave thanks for five loaves of bread and two fish. He satisfied over 5,000 people with this lunch. Nothing is impossible with God!

Memory Verse

They all ate and were satisfied.

Matthew 14:20

Directions

1. Copy and cut out the patterns on page 104. Color the Jesus pattern and glue it to the top half of a dinner-size plate (eating side).

2. To make a basket, cut a second dinner-size plate in half. Color the basket with a basket weave design. Glue around the inside rim of the basket, leaving a 1" (2.5 cm) space unglued at the bottom (fig. 1). Place the glued half, rim to rim, (eating sides facing inward) to the plate with the Jesus pattern. Keep the rims together with paper clips until dry (fig. 2).

3. Color the individual fish and loaf patterns and glue them onto the other half of the plate that made the basket. Cut out the patterns and glue them to the underside of the basket. Leave just a small portion of each pattern showing above the basket (fig. 3).

4. Color the grouped fish and loaves pattern and glue it to the center of a dessert size paper plate. Cut out the pattern and glue a jumbo craft stick to the back of the fish and loaves pattern (fig. 4).

5. Drop the fish and loaves pattern into the top of the basket so that the stick comes through the opening at the bottom of the basket.

6. Push up the craft stick to fill the basket with more fish and loaves of bread.

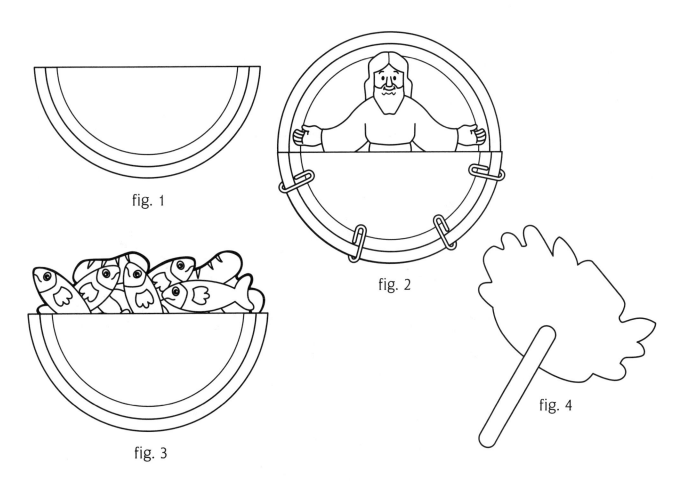

fig. 1

fig. 2

fig. 3

fig. 4

Jesus Feeds the Hungry People Patterns

Jesus Walks on Water

Matthew 14:22-33

Peter walked on water for a short time, but Jesus still called his faith "little." Big faith pleases God! He wants us to trust Him and to do mighty things in His name.

Memory Verse

Immediately Jesus reached out his hand and caught him. "You of little faith," he said, "why did you doubt?"

Matthew 14:31

Materials

- One flexible paper platter
- Crayons, markers, or paints
- Construction paper (white)
- Pencil
- Scissors
- Glue
- Craft stick
- Two small magnets (strong)

Magnet Walk Toy

This toy uses a magnet to reenact Jesus walking on the water.

Suggested Uses

1. Have children repeat the words of Jesus, "You of little faith, why did you doubt?" each time they move Jesus across the water.

2. Have children tell the story in their own words as they use the toy.

Directions

1. Color the right side of the platter to resemble a beach. Color the rest of the platter to resemble water.

2. Copy and cut out the patterns on page 107. Color. Glue the patterns onto white construction paper and cut them out.

3. Glue the Peter pattern onto the left side of the platter. (Do not glue the Jesus figure to the platter.)

4. Glue a magnet to the top of a craft stick and another magnet to the back of the Jesus pattern (figs. 1 and 2). (Be sure to glue the magnets so that they attract rather than repel each other.)

5. Hold the stick under the platter and guide Jesus across the water to rescue Peter.

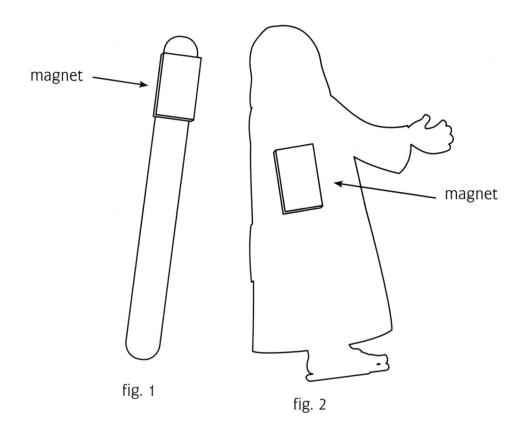

magnet

fig. 1

magnet

fig. 2

Jesus Walks on Water Patterns

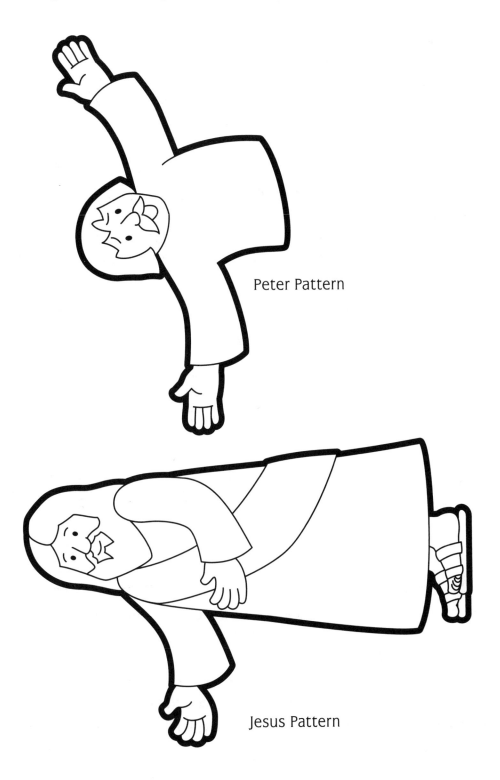

Peter Pattern

Jesus Pattern

Garden of Gethsemane

Dry Dish Garden

This garden illustrates the place of suffering where Jesus went to pray the night before He was crucified.

Suggested Uses

1. Allow children to explain how they chose to arrange their garden.
2. Have children use the gardens for table decorations or as gifts.

After the Passover meal, Jesus went to the garden of Gethsemane to pray. Knowing what He was about to suffer gave Him great sorrow. God sent an angel from heaven to give Him strength. God will also give you strength when you are in need.

Memory Verse

[Jesus] went away a second time and prayed, "My Father, if it is not possible for this cup to be taken away unless I drink it, may your will be done."

Matthew 26:42

Materials

- One sturdy paper plate or platter
- Scissors
- Pencil
- Crayons, markers, or paints
- Poster board (various colors)
- Construction paper (various colors)
- Glue

Optional Landscape Materials

Treetops: Glue on cotton balls for foliage. Paint the cotton balls green by rubbing them with a green marker. For a fruit tree, glue on fruits cut from construction paper.

Boulder: painted crumpled paper

Grass: bits of green tissue or crumpled green tissue, crushed crepe paper, finely shredded Easter grass, bits of green construction paper, or curled paper ribbon

Dried Grass: sawdust, packing straw, or slivers of yellow construction paper

Moss: clothes dryer lint or floral moss

Flowers: tiny plastic or silk flowers

Ground covers: sand, sieved soil, dried coffee grounds, sawdust

Directions

1. Plan your garden carefully. Gather the optional landscape materials you may want to use in your garden to go along with your stand-up cutouts.

2. Copy the patterns on page 110. Cut out the patterns and glue them onto poster board.

3. Arrange the patterns and the optional landscape materials on a large dinner plate or platter in an interesting arrangement. When you have decided on an arrangement, fold back the tabs and glue the patterns in place (fig. 1). Glue the other materials in place.

4. Once the stand-ups and other objects are glued in place, coat the inside of the plate or platter with a generous layer of glue and sprinkle or press on some of the optional ground covers. You may prefer to paint a ground cover instead.

fig. 1

Garden of Gethsemane Patterns

Jesus Arose

Matthew 28:1-7

Mary Magdalene went to look at Jesus' tomb. She saw that the stone placed over its entrance was rolled back and an angel was there. The angel said, "Jesus is not here; he has risen, just as he said." Celebrate this joyful event every day and especially on Resurrection Sunday.

Memory Verse

"He is not here; he has risen, just as he said."

Matthew 28:6

Dry Dish Garden

This garden illustrates the joyful day when Jesus arose.

Suggested Uses

1. Have children use their gardens for table decorations to celebrate Easter.

2. Have children tell others about the story they depicted in their gardens.

Materials

- One sturdy paper plate or platter
- Scissors
- Pencil
- Crayons, markers, or paints
- Poster board (various colors)
- Construction paper (various colors)
- Glue

Optional Landscape Materials

Treetops: Paint cotton balls green by rubbing them with a green marker. For a fruit tree, glue on fruits cut from construction paper.

Mountain: driftwood, small rock, or textured tree bark from fallen tree

Grass: bits of green tissue or crumpled green tissue, crushed crepe paper, finely shredded Easter grass, bits of green construction paper, or curled paper ribbon

Dried Grass: sawdust, packing straw, or slivers of yellow construction paper

Moss: clothes dryer lint or floral moss

Flowers: tiny plastic or silk flowers

Butterfly: Cut a tiny butterfly from tissue paper. Glue it to a toothpick and place among the flowers.

Tomb: painted crumpled paper

Ground covers: sand, sieved soil, sawdust

Directions

1. Plan your garden carefully. Gather the optional landscape materials you may want to use in your garden to go along with your stand-up cutouts.

2. Copy the patterns on page 113. Cut out the patterns and glue them onto poster board.

3. Arrange the patterns and the optional landscape materials on a large dinner plate or platter in an interesting arrangement. When you have decided on an arrangement, fold back the tabs and glue the patterns in place (fig. 1). Glue the other materials in place.

4. Once the stand-ups and other objects are glued in place, coat the inside of the plate or platter with a generous layer of glue and sprinkle or press on some of the optional ground covers. You may prefer to paint a ground cover instead.

fig. 1

Jesus Arose Patterns

Soar with Jesus

Discus

Matthew 28:16-20

Throw the discus and spread the good news of Jesus.

Suggested Uses

1. Have children draw a religious symbol of their choice on the discus, then explain what the symbol means to them.

2. Have children toss the discus back and forth as they recite the memory verse.

Jesus told His disciples to go and make disciples of all nations. Be a disciple of Jesus and teach others the Word of God.

Memory Verse

"Go and make disciples of all nations."

Matthew 28:19

Materials

- Two sturdy dinner-size paper plates
- Glue
- Pencil
- Crayons, markers, or paints

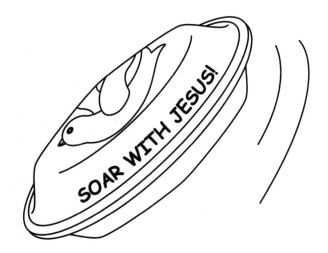

Directions

1. Glue two sturdy dinner-size plates together, rim-to-rim (with the eating sides facing inward).

2. Write "Soar with Jesus" around the edge of the discus.

3. Color both sides of the discus.

4. Copy and cut out the dove pattern below. Color the pattern and glue it onto the discus.

I Am a New Creation!

Wave the wand and watch the butterfly soar though the air.

Suggested Uses

1. Have children repeat, "I am a new creation!" as they fly their butterflies.

2. Allow children to fly the butterflies during a special service.

Materials

- One flexible dinner-size paper plate
- Pencil
- Scissors
- Crayons, markers, or paints
- Glue
- String
- Ruler
- Paper clips
- Construction paper (white)
- One 12" (30 cm) wooden dowel

Remind children of the life cycle of the butterfly. A butterfly egg becomes a caterpillar. The caterpillar spins a cocoon then emerges from it as a butterfly that delights us with its flight and beautiful colors. Let the transformed life of the butterfly remind children that when we accept Jesus in our hearts, God makes us righteous in His sight. This transforms us into a new creation!

Memory Verse

If anyone is in Christ, he is a new creation; the old has gone, the new has come!

2 Corinthians 5:17

Directions

1. Fold a flexible dinner-size paper plate in half to locate its center.

2. Copy and cut out the butterfly pattern on page 118.

3. Place the pattern along the fold of the eating side of the plate. Use a pencil to trace the outline of the butterfly pattern. Turn the pattern to the other side of the fold and trace again (fig. 1).

4. Cut out the butterfly and color the wings with colorful designs.

5. Glue along the inside fold of the butterfly. Place one end of a 36" (90 cm) string along the fold (fig. 2).

6. Fold the butterfly so that the two sides of the body (not the wings) are glued together with the string enclosed. Hold in place with paper clips until dry (fig. 3).

7. Cut a 0.25" x 12" (0.6 cm x 30 cm) strip of construction paper for the antennae. Curl the ends of the strip by wrapping them around a pencil. Fold the strip in half and glue its center to the fold at the top of the head (fig. 4).

8. Tie the other end of the string to the end of the wooden dowel. Place a dab of glue on the top of the knot for added strength.

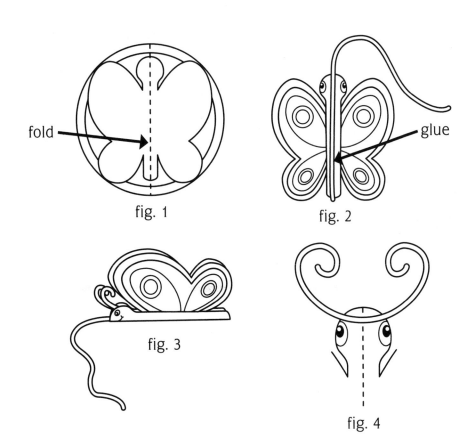

fold

fig. 1

glue

fig. 2

fig. 3

fig. 4

I Am a New Creation! Pattern

Jesus Loves a Cheerful Giver

2 Corinthians 9:6-9

Discover the benefits of being a cheerful giver by reading 2 Corinthians 9:8. Tell children to listen carefully for the word "**all**" and to repeat it loudly, opening their arms wide each time they hear it.

*And God is able to make **all** grace abound to you, so that in **all** things at **all** times, having **all** that you need, you will abound in every good work.*

Memory Verse

God loves a cheerful giver.

2 Corinthians 9:7

Materials

- Two sturdy paper bowls
- Crayons, markers, or paints
- Pencil
- Scissors
- Glue
- Paper clip
- Pictures cut from Sunday school leaflets, old greeting cards, magazines, calendars, or postcards
- Two brass paper fasteners
- Thin ribbon
- Candy or small toys

Caution: Before distributing candies, ask families' permission and inquire about students' food allergies and religious or other food preferences.

Caution: Small toys can present a choking hazard for children under three years.

Gift Box

Fill this pretty box with small gifts or candies and give it to a friend!

Suggested Uses

1. Allow children to take their boxes home to give to a friend or family member, or distribute them as a group to home-bound church members or nursing home residents.

2. Have children write prayers to include in the gift boxes or enclose gift tags with spiritual messages.

Directions

1. Turn two sturdy paper bowls upside down and color the bottoms and sides.
2. Cut one of the bowls to make a 1.5" (3.8 cm) hinge (fig. 1).
3. Bend up the hinge along the bowl's bottom edge (fig. 2).
4. Glue just the hinge to the rim of the other bowl (fig. 3). Hold in place with a paper clip until dry.
5. Glue pictures or stickers to the top of the box lid. Or, draw and color pictures.
6. Insert a brass paper fastener into the front edge of each bowl. Tie a piece of thin ribbon around one of the fasteners. To keep the lid closed, tie the ribbon to the other fastener.

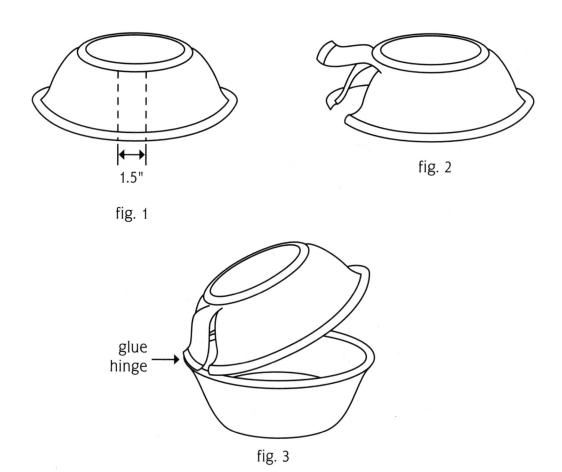

1.5"

fig. 1

fig. 2

glue hinge →

fig. 3

Open Your Heart to Jesus

Colossians 3:12–15

Remind children that Jesus is always patient and kind with them. Since His Holy Spirit lives in their hearts, they can show God's patience and kindness to others. God's love was put in our hearts to share!

Memory Verse

Let the peace of Christ rule in your hearts.

Colossians 3:15

This heart-shaped card reveals a figure of Jesus.

Suggested Uses

1. Use the cards as invitations to special services, meetings, or parties.

2. Have children write special messages on the cards for Valentine's Day.

Materials

- Two flexible dinner-size paper plates
- Crayons, markers, or paints
- Scissors
- Pencil
- Glue
- Paper hole punch
- Yarn

closed card   open card

Directions

1. Color just the rim on both sides of a flexible dinner-size plate. Fold the plate in half (eating sides facing inward) and crease.

2. With the plate folded, cut around the edge so that when the plate is opened it becomes a heart shape (figs. 1 and 2).

3. Write "Open Your ♥ to Jesus!" on one side of the folded heart. (See closed card illustration on page 121.)

4. Copy and cut out the Jesus pattern on page 123. Glue the pattern onto a second flexible dinner-size plate or construction paper. Color and cut out.

5. Fold the Jesus pattern in half and crease (fig. 3).

6. On the back of the Jesus pattern, place a drop of glue at the outer corners of the robe and at the ends of the sleeves on each side of the pattern (fig. 4). Open the heart and center the pattern over the fold of the heart. (Let the glue dry thoroughly before closing the heart.)

7. Decorate the greeting card.

8. Close the heart and use a paper hole punch to make two holes in the outer edge of the heart. Thread a piece of yarn through the holes and tie a bow. (See the closed card illustration on page 121.)

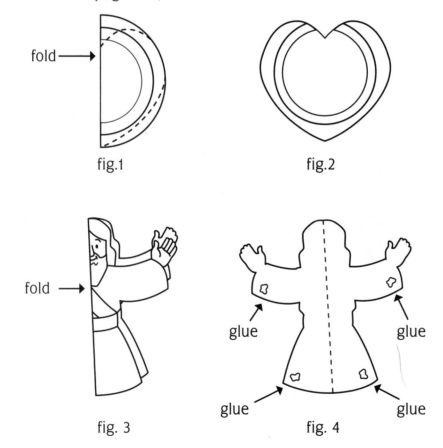

fig.1 fig.2

fold

fig. 3 glue glue glue glue fig. 4

Open Your Heart to Jesus Pattern

Bible Story Theater and Puppets

Multi-Use Project

Use this backdrop to tell various stories from the Bible.

Suggested Uses

1. Use the Bible character puppet patterns in this book to act out Bible stories.

2. Write skits and perform puppet shows.

Materials

- Two sturdy dinner size paper plates
- Ruler
- Pencil
- Scissors
- Jumbo craft stick
- Crayons, markers, or paints
- Glue
- Poster board (white)
- Craft sticks or plastic drinking straws (one for each puppet)

John's Gospel ends with the words of this memory verse. As children choose Bible stories to tell using the Bible Story Theater, remind them that Jesus did many other wonderful things that were not written down.

Memory Verse

Jesus did many other things as well. If every one of them were written down, I suppose that even the whole world would not have room for the books that would be written.

John 21:25

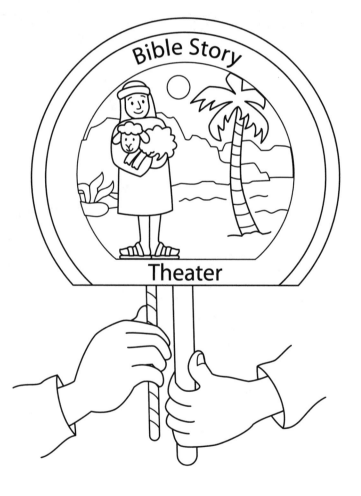

Directions

1. Cut 1" (2.5 cm) from the bottom of a dinner-size plate (fig. 1). Put this plate inside a second dinner-size plate and use a pencil to trace the cut edge. Remove the plate and cut along the traced line to make both plates the same shape.

2. Color a background scene for the theater on the eating side of one plate.

3. On the other plate, cut an opening for the theater. Do not cut through the rim or bottom edge (fig. 2).

4. Glue the plates together, rim-to-rim (with eating sides facing inward) (fig. 3). This gives an opening to put the puppets on stage.

5. Glue a jumbo craft stick to the back of the theater for a handle.

6. To make stick puppets, draw Bible characters and animals on poster board. Be sure to make the puppets small enough to fit inside the theater. Color and cut out the puppets.

7. Glue a craft stick or a plastic drinking straw to the back of each puppet for a handle.

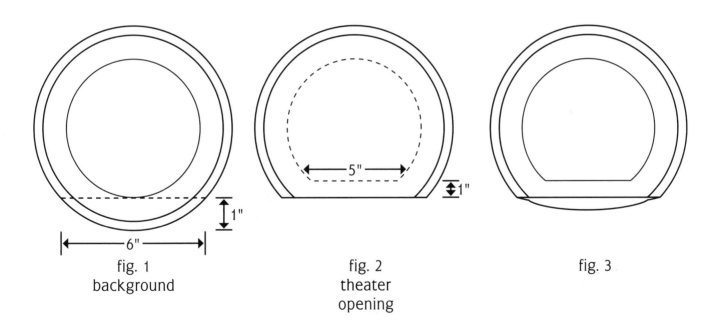

fig. 1
background

fig. 2
theater
opening

fig. 3

Angel Messenger

Multi-Use Hand Puppet

This angel with its flapping wings can be used to tell many Bible stories.

Suggested Uses

1. Have children tell stories in which angels appear as God's messengers:

   Elijah in the Wilderness
   1 Kings 19:1–8

   Daniel in the Lions' Den
   Daniel 6:22

   Birth of John the Baptist
   Luke 1:5–20

   Birth of Jesus
   Luke 2:13–14

   Jesus' Resurrection
   Matthew 28:5–7

2. Allow children to take their angels home to use as Christmas decorations.

Materials

- Two flexible dinner-size paper plates
- Pencil
- Scissors
- Crayons, markers, or paints
- Glue
- Paper clips

Optional Trim Materials

Cord (gold or silver), paper doilies (white, gold, or silver, metallic rickrack, tinsel, glitter glue, sequins

Angels are a special class of beings. They serve God in Heaven and on Earth by ministering to believers. They are usually invisible, but sometimes appear in angelic form or disguised as humans. Even though they may sometimes appear as human (Hebrews 13:2) they don't become human, and humans do not become angels when they go to Heaven. Explain to children that as believers, they have angels charged to protect them and to minister to their needs.

Memory Verse

Are not all angels ministering spirits sent to serve those who will inherit salvation?

Hebrews 1:14

Directions

1. Copy and cut out the angel pattern on page 128. Glue the pattern onto the non-eating side of a flexible dinner-size plate. The rest of the plate (around the angel) makes up the fronts of the wings and the halo.

2. Color the angel. Decorate the plate around the angel pattern to resemble wings. Apply optional decorative trims as desired. Leave a portion at the top blank to resemble a halo.

3. Fold the angel in half (pressing the wings together) with the angel on the inside of the fold.

4. To make the backs of the wings, cut a second flexible dinner-size plate in half. Then, cut 1" (2.5 cm) from the cut edge of each half (fig. 1).

5. Glue the cut halves to the angel plate, rim-to-rim (with eating sides facing inward), to form a pocket on each side of the fold. Hold in place with paper clips until dry.

6. To make the angel's wings flap, slip your hand inside the pockets and open and close your hand (fig. 2).

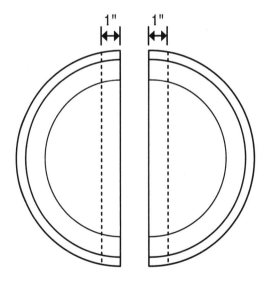

fig. 1

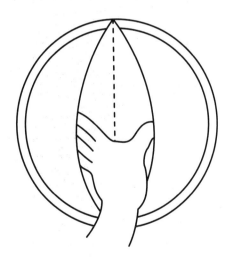

fig. 2

Angel Messenger Pattern